BRITAIN IRELAND and EUROPE from 1570 - 1745

N. Johnston ∎ A. Hodge ∎ R. Rees ∎ A. Logan

2nd Edition
Edited by A. Hodge

COLOURPOINT PRESS

The Colourpoint Logo
The Colourpoint is one of the most beautiful of all the long-haired cat breeds. Persian in temperament and shape, it has the coloured points of the Siamese on the face, ears, paws and tail. The Colourpoint logo depicts a real blue-cream point kitten, Lady Jane Grey, and was drawn by Rhoda McClure, a fifth form art student at Omagh Academy, Co. Tyrone

© N. Johnston
   A. Hodge
   R. Rees
   A. Logan
   1994

First published by the
Western Education and
Library Board, 1992

Second edition published
by Colourpoint Press,
1994

ISBN 1 898392 04 8

All rights reserved. No part of this publication may be reproduced, stored in a retrieval system or transmitted in any form by any means, electronic, mechanical, photocopying, recording or otherwise, without the prior written permission of the copyright owners and publisher of this book.

Layout and design: Sheila Johnston
Map design: Norman Johnston
Original cover concept: MainStreet, Hillsborough, Co. Down
Typeset by: Colourpoint Press
Film output and map production by: TypeForm Repro, Dublin
Printed by ColourBooks, Dublin

Cover illustrations:

Top — Treasure from the Girona, wrecked off the coast of Co Antrim near the Giant's Causeway on the 28th October 1588.

Bottom — Keep and interior of Bawn at Clonony, Co Offaly, built as part of the Laois-Offaly Plantation of 1556.

The Authors
Norman Johnston, Audrey M. Hodge and Russell Rees are all members of the History Department at Omagh Academy, Co. Tyrone. They have many years' experience of teaching the Northern Ireland curriculum. Audrey Hodge and Russell Rees are joint authors of *Ireland and British Politics from 1870-1921*, published by Colourpoint in 1993.
Austin Logan has a B.A. (Hons) in European and Irish History, an M.A. in History and Education and a Ph.D. in Approaches to Teaching and Learning. He has designed classroom materials, written articles on the teaching of history, and is Advisor for Environment and Society with the Western Education and Library Board.
Norman Johnston graduated from Queen's University with joint honours in History and Politics. He is the author of several church histories and *The Fintona Horse Tram* published by the West Tyrone Historical Society in 1992. He is also the author of *The Norman Impact on the Medieval World* to be published by Colourpoint in 1994.
Audrey Hodge obtained her M.A. in Modern and Contemporary History at the University of Ulster. She is the author of *Gallows and Turnkeys*, a short history of Omagh Gaol.
Russell Rees graduated in History with honours at the University of Ulster and his doctoral thesis dealt with the Northern Ireland problem between 1945 and 1951.

Acknowledgements
The authors and publisher would like to thank the following for permission to reproduce the illustrations listed below:
Ulster Museum, Belfast: Top cover illustration, 30D, 31F, 69A, 70C
National Galleries of Scotland: 15C, 17B, 51B, 67D, 79B.
Hulton Deutsch Collection Ltd: 22A, 25E.
Mary Evans Picture Library: 11A, 13A, 19B, 37D.
A. Candon, Ulster History Park, Omagh: 40A, 44D.
N. Johnston: Lower cover illustration, 72A.
Dept. of the Environment, Historic Monuments Branch: 45E.
A. Hodge: 23B.
Gemma Devlin, Collegiate Grammar School, Enniskillen: 45F.
Dr. W. Maguire: 74A.
W. Winters: 4, 39, 54A, 55B, 55C, 56A, 57C, 58A.

COLOURPOINT PRESS
Omagh Business Complex
Gortrush
Omagh
Co. Tyrone
BT78 5LS

Contents

PART ONE CAUSES OF EUROPEAN RIVALRIES AND CONFLICTS

	Introduction	4
1.1	The Map of Europe in 1570	6
1.2	Religion	8
1.3	The Most Powerful Countries in 1570	10
1.4	A Continent at War	12

CASE STUDY ONE MARY QUEEN OF SCOTS

1.5	Mary's Early Life	14
1.6	Mary, Queen of Scotland	16
1.7	Mary and Elizabeth I	18
1.8	The Death of Mary, Queen of Scots	20

CASE STUDY TWO THE SPANISH ARMADA

1.9	England and Spain	22
1.10	Philip II	24
1.11	The Armada's Voyage	26
1.12	Ireland and the Armada	28

PART TWO THE EXPERIENCE OF COLONISATION AND PLANTATION

2.1	What is a Colony?	32
2.2	Colonies and Trade	34
2.3	The American Colonies	36
2.4	Ireland before the Plantations	38
2.5	Plantation	40
2.6	The Ulster Plantation	42
2.7	Omagh — A Plantation Case Study	46
2.8	The Results of the Ulster Plantation	48

PART THREE POLITICAL AND RELIGIOUS CONFLICT IN BRITAIN

3.1	James I and the Puritans	50
3.2	The Gunpowder Plot	52
3.3	Charles I and Parliament	54
3.4	The English Civil War	56
3.5	Oliver Cromwell	58
3.6	Cromwell's Campaign in Ireland	60
3.7	The Cromwellian Settlement	62

PART FOUR THE WILLIAMITE WARS

4.1	Europe in 1688	64
4.2	James II and Ireland	66
4.3	The Williamite Wars	68
4.4	The Siege of Derry	70
4.5	The Battle of the Boyne	72
4.6	Limerick and Aughrim	74
4.7	The Treaty of Limerick	76
4.8	The Jacobites	78
	Index	80

Introduction

On the fifth day up came a great storm upon our beam, so that our cables could not hold, nor were the sails of any use and all three ships were driven down on a sandy beach surrounded on every side by great rocks ... a most terrible spectacle ... in the space of one hour all the ships were dashed to pieces and not more than 300 men escaped.

More than 1000 were drowned and among them many persons of rank, captains, gentlemen and others .... I commended myself to God and to Our Lady and went aft to the top of the ship's poop and from thence I looked about on the great spectacle of woe. Many men were sinking in the ships; others, throwing themselves into the water went down and never came up; some were on rafts or water casks, captains threw their gold chains and their money into the sea and some gentlemen I saw clinging to mast-spars; others left on the ships cried aloud calling upon God and some were swept off by waves which took them right out of the ships and as I was staring at this horror, I knew not what to do or what part to take, for I cannot swim and the waves and the storm were very great.

This dramatic account of the shipwreck of the Spanish ships **La Lavia** and **Santa Maria de Vision** off the coast of Co Sligo on 25 September 1588 was written by **Francisco De Cuellar**, the captain of one of the ships. These ships, along with the **San Juan**, wrecked on the same date at the same spot, were part of the mighty Spanish Armada. Throughout this book you will read more drama like this, more excitement, rivalry, intrigue, revolution and war. Such is the 'stuff' of history.

For many of you, European history will be a new area of study and Part One sets the scene for those unfamiliar with this exciting period in early modern Europe. The remaining three chapters also correspond to the central themes of the History Study Unit known as 'Core 2'. Each chapter contains text, sources and questions related to the three attainment targets of the National Curriculum. Where difficult phrases or concepts are introduced, these are explained briefly in brackets. The intention throughout the book is to make the period easier for you to understand and more enjoyable to study.

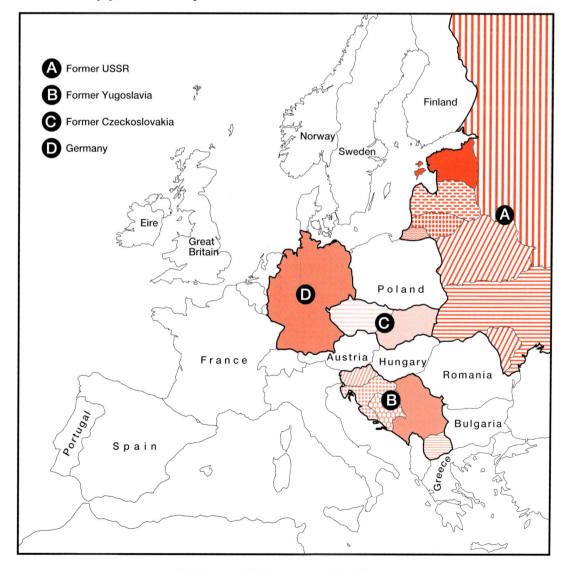

Map of Europe Today

CAUSES OF EUROPEAN RIVALRIES AND ONFLICTS

1.1 The Map of Europe in 1570

The starting point for any study of European history is to look at an historical map and see what Europe looked like at the time. The map of Europe has changed more than that of any other continent. The rise and fall of empires and the ravages of war have frequently changed the boundaries of Europe. Even today this is true. Between the end of the Second World War (1945) and 1989 the political map of Europe scarcely altered. An atlas printed in 1960 was still accurate in 1985. But since 1989 the collapse of communism in eastern Europe has made every map out of date:

> - Germany has been unified
> - The USSR has broken up into a number of independent states
> - Yugoslavia has been split up
> - Czechoslovakia has been divided.

All this means that a school pupil of 2010 looking at a 1985 map of central and eastern Europe will hardly recognise what they see as their Europe of 2010. Yet although things change in history there is also continuity with the past. Look at the map of Europe in 1570 (Source A). Although this shows Europe over 400 years ago you will see a mixture of countries that you recognise and names that are unfamiliar.

ATTAINMENT TARGET 1: CAUSE, CONSEQUENCE AND CHANGE

1.1

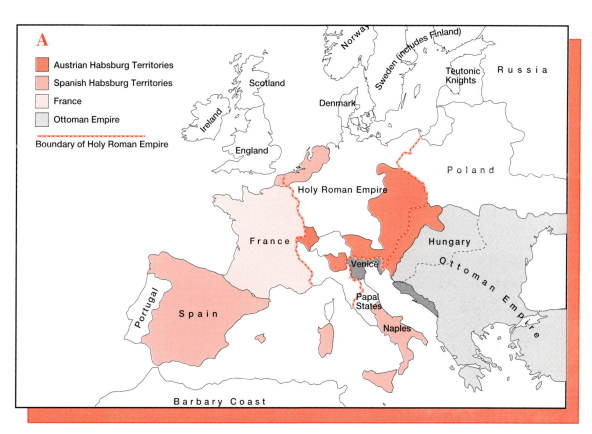

Europe in 1570

The Holy Roman Empire

The Holy Roman Empire was the name given to a large area of central Europe, which included present day Germany, Austria, Switzerland and parts of Northern Italy. It was ruled by the Emperor from the Royal family of Habsburgs.

At the same time the Pope, who lived in Rome, was not just the leader of the Roman Catholic Church but he also owned and ruled over an area of central Italy called the Papal States. For this reason, he was concerned by arguments over land ownership in Europe in this period.

?

1 Which European countries in 1570 are still countries today? (Source A and page 5)

2 Which countries no longer exist?

3 Can you see any other similarities and differences between the two maps?

CAUSES OF EUROPEAN RIVALRIES AND ONFLICTS

1.2 Religion

In the 16th century **religion** was much more important than it is today. It is impossible to understand the rivalries and conflicts of late 16th century Europe without taking religion into account. Broadly speaking there were two main religions in Europe.

CHRISTIAN   Following the teaching of Christ

MOSLEM (Islam) Following the teaching of Mohammed

However, although there was conflict between Christians and Moslems, the main religious divisions were within Christianity. Christians were divided into three main groups:

A

EASTERN ORTHODOX
- Russia
- Ottoman Empire

ROMAN CATHOLIC
- Portugal
- Most of Spain
- Most of France
- Part of Scotland
- Most of Ireland
- South of Holy Roman Empire
- Venice
- Papal States
- Naples
- Hungary
- Poland
- Teutonic Knights

PROTESTANT
- England
- Denmark
- Norway
- Sweden
- Part of France
- Part of Scotland
- Part of Ireland
- North of Holy Roman Empire

MOSLEM
- North Africa and the Barbary Coast
- Parts of the Ottoman Empire
- Southern Spain

Religious divisions in Europe in 1570

ATTAINMENT TARGET 2: POINTS OF VIEW

1.2

Martin Luther and the Reformation

Until **1517** western Europe was **Catholic** and eastern Europe **Eastern Orthodox**. In that year **Martin Luther**, a German monk (Germany was in the Holy Roman Empire) began the religious movement called **the Reformation**. This movement caused a split in the Catholic church into two rival, and often hostile, religious groups - Protestant and Roman Catholic.

In the middle ages the main religious wars in Europe had been between Christians and Moslems. The Moslems had conquered the whole of north Africa, including the Barbary Coast, and in the early 15th century ruled southern Spain. The Turks had extended their Ottoman Empire into southern Europe and had penetrated deep into Hungary. In the 16th century the European part of the Ottoman Empire was an uneasy mix of Moslems and Eastern Orthodox Christians.

However, in the period we are studying (the late 16th century) the Christian/Moslem rivalry had been overtaken by the bitter divisions developing in western Europe between Catholic and Protestant states. These divisions were particularly acute within the Holy Roman Empire (modern Germany, Austria, Switzerland, etc).

?

1. Which religious groups could be found in (a) Ottoman Empire (b) Ireland (c) Norway (d) Holy Roman Empire?

2. How does Source A help to explain that there may be religious rivalries among the people of the Ottoman Empire and the Holy Roman Empire?

3. Suggest reasons why religion was important to people then.

CAUSES OF EUROPEAN RIVALRIES AND CONFLICTS

1.3 The Most Powerful Countries in 1570

ACTIVITIES

1. Discuss with a partner, or in small groups, the factors which make a country powerful. Put them in order and discuss your reasons.
2. Compare your group's answers with the rest of the class. Try to come to class agreement on their order of importance.
3. Using these criteria place, Spain, France and the Holy Roman Empire in order of importance.

Let us consider what makes one country more powerful than another. Three factors are particularly important:

(a) **Geographical size**   Compare the Holy Roman Empire with Venice (look at Source A in Unit 1.1)

(b) **Population**   A larger population allowed a ruler to have a bigger army which gave him more power.

(c) **Wealth**   Trade made several countries very rich. This could compensate for being small in size or population. For this reason England and Venice, although small, could afford to have powerful navies. Spain and Portugal had overseas empires in America.

In eastern Europe the most powerful states were Sweden, Poland, Russia and the Ottoman Empire. We are mainly concerned with western Europe in which three states were powerful in 1570.

SPAIN

Ruler: Philip II (1556-1598).
Religion: Catholic.
Economy: Mainly agriculture. Immense wealth due to imported silver from central and southern America (The New World).
Armed Forces: Large navy and powerful army.
Politics: Rival of France. Controlled the Low Countries (Holland and Belgium).

FRANCE

Ruler: Charles IX (1560-1574)
Religion: Mainly Catholic but some Protestants
Economy: Agriculture, trade and industry
Armed Forces: Good army and navy
Politics: Rival of Spain

HOLY ROMAN EMPIRE

Ruler: Maximilian II (1564-1576).
Religion: Catholic and Protestant.
Economy: Agriculture, trade and industry.
Armed Forces: Each state had its own army.
Politics: Maximilian was an Emperor ruling a loose federation (group) of independent states. The Empire had little real unity.

ATTAINMENT TARGET 1: CAUSE, CONSEQUENCE AND CHANGE

1.3

Philip II, King of Spain

> **?**
>
> 1 Look at the three factors which make a country powerful. Which do you consider to be the most important and why?
>
> 2 Examine the portrait of Philip II (Source A). How does this portrait illustrate the fact that Philip was a man of great power?

CAUSES OF EUROPEAN RIVALRIES AND CONFLICTS

1.4 A Continent at War

Western Europe had been at war for most of the sixteenth century. There were three types of war going on:

(a) Dynastic Wars

Each European state was ruled by a royal family (dynasty) which handed the crown on from father to son or to the next male heir if there was no son. The importance of any king or emperor was judged by the amount of land or number of territories he ruled over. Each dynasty tried to add to its territories either by marriage or conquest. Since England had a Queen, **Philip II** of Spain was keen to marry **Elizabeth I** so that England could be added to his dominions.

The most powerful family in Europe were the **Habsburgs**. **Charles V (1519-1556)** was Holy Roman Emperor, but his personal dominions included Austria, most of Italy, the Netherlands, part of France, Spain and the New World (America).

The main challenge to Habsburg power was the **Valois dynasty** in France. Several times before 1570 there were wars between the Habsburgs and the Valois kings. These wars drew in other European countries as well. **Scotland** usually supported France and before 1558 **England** supported Spain. These alliances were often cemented by marriage. **Mary Queen of Scots** married **Francis II** of France (1559-60). **Henry VIII** of England married a Spanish princess, Katherine of Aragon, and their daughter **Mary I** of England (1553-58) married the Habsburg **Philip II** of Spain (1556-98). When she died Philip tried to marry her sister **Elizabeth I**.

(b) Civil Wars

Civil wars are wars **within** a country as distinct from wars **between** countries. Between 1562 and 1598 France was embroiled in a series of bitter internal civil wars between the French nobles and the Valois kings. These wars were also partly religious. Many of the nobles were Protestants (the French called them **Huguenots**). In **1572** there was a general massacre of Protestants in Paris and some of the provinces (see Source A). It is estimated that between 6000 and 50,000 were murdered in a matter of days, in the **St Bartholomew's Day** massacre.

ATTAINMENT TARGET 3: USE OF EVIDENCE

The massacre of St Bartholemew, This event took place on 24th August 1572

(c) Religious Wars

The **Reformation** (1517) had caused a bitter division in Europe between Catholics and Protestants. Religion was a major factor in breaking up the traditional alliance between England and Spain. Within the Holy Roman Empire the rulers of some German states became Protestant, but others remained Catholic.

In **1545** the Catholic church began a belated attempt to stem the rising tide of Protestantism. The **Council of Trent** began meeting in that year to reform the Catholic church and remove abuses that were encouraging conversion to Protestantism. In **1534** a priest called **Ignatius Loyola** founded the **Society of Jesus** (Jesuits) as a missionary order to reconvert people in the Protestant countries. In countries which had very few Protestants the **Inquisition** (a sort of religious court) was used to stamp out all signs of **heresy** (deviation from Christian teaching). The Inquisition could use torture and burning at the stake, and was very successful in Spain and Italy. In the late 16th century most wars had a religious element to them.

?

1. Explain the meaning of the following terms: dynasty; dominions; Habsburgs; Reformation; Jesuit; Inquisition; Huguenot.

2. What does Source A tell us about the massacre?

3. How useful are pictures such as Source A to an historian? Explain your answer.

CASE STUDY ONE: MARY, QUEEN OF SCOTS

1.5 Mary's Early Life

Mary Queen of Scots was born in Scotland in 1542, the daughter of the Scottish **King James V** and his Queen, a French princess, **Mary of Guise.** James was already near death, worn out by the intrigues of France, England and his own noblemen. He died when Mary was less than a week old. When he received the news of her birth he recalled how the throne had come to his family through Margery Bruce. *"It came with a lass, and it will gang with a lass."* Then he laughed and fell back dead! Mary was Queen of Scotland, perhaps History's youngest Queen. She was to live for 45 years - a turbulent and troubled life of disastrous marriages, intrigues, murders, plots and eventually imprisonment and execution.

Mary's early life

Mary of Guise tried to rule Scotland as **regent** (ruler of a kingdom if the person supposed to rule is too young or is absent) for her young daughter. She sent Mary to live in France at the age of six (1548) when she was betrothed (engaged) to **Francis**, the four year old son of the French king **Henry II**. They were married ten years later in 1558. Shortly after, Henry II was killed in a tournament accident and Francis became King (1559). Mary was **Queen of France**. Her glory was short-lived, however, as her young husband was sickly and died in 1560. At the age of 18 Mary was a widow. Back in Scotland her mother had also died in 1560. No longer Queen of France, Mary decided to return to Scotland in 1561.

A

She had a marvellous way of talking — gentle and feminine, and with kindly majesty. Her speech was modest and reserved, and very graceful. When she spoke Scottish (which is a very barbarous, ill-sounding and rough language) she made it sound beautiful and pleasant — which no one else can.

Brantôme — a French writer of about 1558.

Francis, aged about 14

ACTIVITY

1. Construct a timeline of Mary's life from her birth in 1542 until her death in 1587. Using the information in this unit, fill it in until 1561.

ATTAINMENT TARGET 1: CAUSE, CONSEQUENCE AND CHANGE

Mary, Queen of Scots

D

To promote a woman to bear rule, dominion or empire over any realm, nation or city is repugnant to nature and contumely [insulting] to God. It is a thing most contrary to his revealed will and approved ordinance [decree]. Finally it is the subversion of good order, equity and justice.

from *The First Blast of the Trumpet Against the Monstrous Regiment of Women*, John Knox, 1558.

The Reformation in Scotland

Inside Scotland things had been changing. The old alliance with France was no longer popular. England had become Protestant and in Scotland many of the noblemen had converted to Protestantism, including Mary's half-brother **James Stewart**. (Mary used the French version of her name - Stuart). They now wanted Scotland to be allied to England, rather than Catholic France. The Reformation in England had been briefly halted during the reign of Mary I (1553-58), who was Roman Catholic. (This was Mary Tudor, not to be confused with Mary Queen of Scots.) But in 1558 the Protestant, Elizabeth I (1558-1603) had become Queen of England. The Scottish nobles did not want a Catholic Queen, and Mary Queen of Scots was a practising Catholic. As soon as Mary arrived in Scotland there was opposition. The fiercest opposition came from **John Knox**, a fiery Protestant preacher, who was highly critical of Mary. He gave her strong advice on how she should dress and who she should marry. He obviously did not like women to be in a position of authority, as Source D shows.

?

1 What are the differences between the views of Brantôme and John Knox regarding Mary? (Sources A and D)

2 Explain why these two men may have viewed Mary differently.

CASE STUDY ONE: MARY, QUEEN OF SCOTS

1.6 Mary, Queen of Scotland

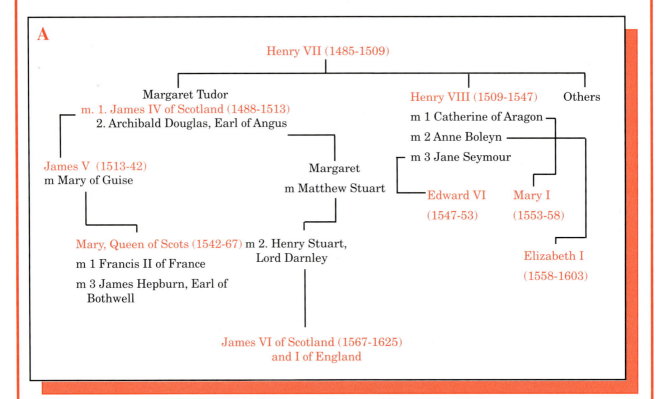

The Relationship between the Tudors and Stuarts (simplified)

The next eight years were the most important in Mary's life. Scandal seemed to pursue her wherever she went. Mary did not persecute the Protestants, but she remained Catholic herself. In 1565 she married **Henry, Lord Darnley,** a handsome 18 year old Roman Catholic, who was also her cousin. They had a son who became **James VI** of Scotland and later **James I** of England. The marriage strengthened Mary's claim to the English throne. She and her husband were both grandchildren of Henry VIII's sister **Margaret Tudor**. Darnley was proclaimed King of Scotland ruling alongside Mary.

The Murder of Rizzio

Darnley turned out to be lazy, arrogant and spoilt. In 1566 he led a plot to murder **David Rizzio** the Queen's Italian secretary and musician. Armed men burst into the Queen's apartment and dragged Rizzio screaming into the hall where he was stabbed and hacked to death. The body suffered 56 stab wounds. Darnley was convinced that Rizzio was Mary's secret lover.

Mary stayed with Darnley until their son James was born, but she had now fallen in love with the **Earl of Bothwell**, a dashing young soldier. On 9 February 1567 Darnley was lying ill at a house on the outskirts of Edinburgh called **Kirk O'Fields**. The house was blown up and the

> **ACTIVITY**
>
> Add to your timeline the important dates in Mary's life as related in this unit.

ATTAINMENT TARGET 3: USE OF EVIDENCE

1.6

The Murder of Rizzio, painted by Sir William Allan in 1833

?

1 Source B was painted in 1833, 267 years after the event took place. Is it reliable as evidence? Explain your answer.

2 Why do you think source C was produced?

3 How may the answer to question 2 affect the reliability of Source C?

body of both Darnley and his servant were found strangled in the garden (Source C). Rumours swept Edinburgh that Bothwell and even the Queen were involved in the murder of Darnley. Despite this, Mary married Bothwell three months later. This led to an immediate rebellion. Mary was captured, imprisoned in **Lochleven Castle** and her infant son James proclaimed **James VI**. But Mary escaped in May 1568 and arrived in England to throw herself on the mercy of **Elizabeth I**.

Print showing Darnley's body at Kirk O'Fields, 1567

17

CASE STUDY ONE: MARY, QUEEN OF SCOTS

1.7 Mary and Elizabeth I

The arrival of Mary Queen of Scots in England caused major problems for Queen Elizabeth I.

- She could hardly refuse political sanctuary (a safe place to stay) for her cousin.
- Since Elizabeth was unmarried and had no children, Mary was her heir. Elizabeth was 35 and might yet marry, of course.
- The French had recognised Mary as **Queen of England**. See family tree page 16. Because Catholics did not believe **Henry VIII** was legitimately married to his second wife **Anne Boleyn**, they regarded Elizabeth as the daughter of his mistress and so not entitled to be Queen. Thus to Catholics, Mary Queen of Scots was the rightful heir of **Mary I** (Mary Tudor).
- If Mary was allowed to live in England unrestricted, English Catholics might be tempted to make Mary Queen and thus rebel against Elizabeth.
- Mary's son James was being brought up as a Protestant. If Elizabeth sent Mary back to Scotland it could result in a Catholic Queen north of the border, instead of a Protestant King. Alternatively, the Scots might kill Mary.
- If she sent Mary to France, Catholic powers might invade England in an attempt to make Mary Queen.
- The easy way out might be to execute Mary - but on what grounds? She had committed no crime in England. In any case if a Queen executed another Queen it might set a precedent (an example that others might copy).

A

We declare the aforesaid Elizabeth to be excommunicated by the Church. Moreover we declare that Elizabeth's title as Queen of England is false. No English nobles or subjects need keep their promises of loyalty or obedience to her. No one may obey her orders ...

Papal Bull, 1570. To be excommunicated means to be deprived of any right to the services of the Church, and thereby doomed to spend eternity in Hell.

ACTIVITIES

1 In groups, construct a prosecution and a defence case for Mary, Queen of Scots, who is accused of treason. One representative from each group is to put their 'case' to the rest of the class.

2 (a) Write a letter from Mary, Queen of Scots to Elizabeth, protesting her innocence and asking for Elizabeth's sympathy and help.

(b) Write a letter from Elizabeth to her most trusted adviser, explaining her dilemma about how to deal with Mary.

ATTAINMENT TARGET 2: POINTS OF VIEW

1.7

Elizabeth was careful never to meet Mary face to face. Instead she had the charges against Mary investigated, but the investigation neither proved Mary guilty of involvement in Darnley's murder, nor innocent either. Mary was allowed to stay in England as a 'guest' of Elizabeth, but in reality she was a prisoner, held at various castles against her will. During this time Mary was the focus of a number of plots against Elizabeth. This was a dangerous time for Elizabeth internationally. Catholic **Spain** was now an enemy of England, and Elizabeth was secretly aiding Protestants in the **Netherlands** who were rebelling against Spain. **The Pope** regarded Elizabeth as a heretic and in 1570 issued a **Bull** (statement carrying the full authority of the Church). Part of this is reproduced in Source A.

Queen Elizabeth I

1 How can we tell from Source A that the threat to Elizabeth I's position from her Catholic subjects would be increased?

2 Why do you think that Elizabeth would never agree to meet Mary?

CASE STUDY ONE: MARY, QUEEN OF SCOTS

1.8 The Death of Mary, Queen of Scots

From this time on the number of plots involving Mary increased and in 1572 Parliament brought charges against her (Source A). Below are some of the plots and events of the period.

A

i. That she has wickedly and untruly challenged the present estate and possession of the crown of England and ... usurped the style and arms of the same.

ii. That she has ... sought by subtle means to withdraw the late Duke of Norfolk from his natural obedience and against Her Majesty's express prohibition to couple herself in marriage with the said Duke, to the intent that thereby she might ... bring to effect Her Majesty's ... destruction.

iii. That she has ... stirred... the Earls of Northumberland and Westmoreland ... to rebel and levy open war against Her Majesty.

iv. That she has practised ... to procure new rebellion to be raised within this realm. And for that intent she made choice of one Ridolphi, a merchant of Italy, who ... solicited the said wicked enterprises to the Pope and other ... confederates beyond the seas.

Charges made by Parliament against Mary, Queen of Scots in May 1572.

1571 **Ridolfi Plot**. Ridolfi (an Italian) planned to marry Mary to the **Duke of Norfolk**, and replace Elizabeth with her. In 1572 Norfolk who was a Roman Catholic, was beheaded.

1572 **St Bartholomew's Day Massacre** in France. This was begun by the Guises, Mary's French relatives.

1584 Assassination of **William of Orange** the Protestant ruler of the Netherlands. This frightened the English government, who wanted Mary to be executed.

Elizabeth could not bring herself to harm Mary, so **Sir Francis Walsingham** (Elizabeth's secretary) set up a trap for her. A young Catholic **Anthony Babington** was persuaded to pass secret messages from Mary to a continental 'agent' (who was in fact a spy for Walsingham). The code for the messages is shown in Source B. When the trap was sprung there was enough proof to find both Babington and Mary Queen of Scots guilty of treason.

Mary was tried in October 1586 at **Fotheringay Castle**, but it was February 1587 before Elizabeth was persuaded to sign the death warrant. The execution took place on 8 February at Fotheringay. Source C is a contemporary account of the event.

B

| a | b | c | d | e | f | g | h | i | k | l | m |
| o | ǂ | △ | ⧺ | ɑ | □ | ϙ | ∞ | ı | ð | n | ∥ |

| n | o | p | q | r | s | t | u | x | y | z |
| ø | ▽ | s | m | f | △ | ɛ | c | 7 | 8 | 9 |

One of the codes used in the Babington Plot

ATTAINMENT TARGET 1: CAUSE, CONSEQUENCE AND CHANGE

1.8

C

With a smiling face she turned to her men servants standing upon a bench (behind the platform). *They were weeping. The Queen bid them farewell.*

She kneeled down upon a cushion and prayed. Then, groping for the block with both her hands, she held them there. They would have been cut off had they not been espied (seen). *Then she laid herself upon the block, most quietly. It took two strokes of the axe before he* (the executioner) *cut off her head. Then one espied a little dog which was under the [dead queen's] clothes. It could not be gotten out by force and afterwards would not depart the dead corpse but came and laid by the shoulders.*

A contemporary account of the execution of Mary Queen of Scots by Robert Wyngfield

ACTIVITY

Use the code in Source B to compose a short letter from Babington's continental 'agent' trying to encourage Mary to take part in a plot against Elizabeth.

D

A contemporary drawing of the execution of Mary Queen of Scots in February 1587.

?

1 Rank in order of importance the charges made by parliament against Mary, Queen of Scots in May 1572 (Source A). Give reasons for the order you have chosen.

2 Why did Elizabeth's attitude to Mary change after 1572?

3 What are the similarities between the two accounts of Mary's execution (Sources C and D)?

CASE STUDY TWO: THE SPANISH *A*rmada

1.9 England and Spain

Queen Elizabeth knighting Sir Francis Drake. After the original by the Victorian artist Gilbert

By 1588 England had become one of the greatest naval powers in the world. This in itself was enough to make England and Spain bitter rivals in the second half of the 16th century. The early voyages of discovery to Africa, Asia and the New World (America) had been by Portuguese and Spanish seamen. **Columbus**, who reached America in **1492**, was financed by Spain, though Italian himself. In **1494** Spain and Portugal had signed a Treaty dividing the New World between them. The New World had abundant resources of silver and gold and soon made Spain rich.

After 1550 England began to get in on the act. English seamen began to trade with both west Africa and south America. At first this was peaceful, but in **1567** a Spanish fleet attacked English ships, commanded by **Sir John Hawkins** in **San Juan de Ulua** harbour in Mexico. Henceforth English seamen regarded Spain as an enemy. Whilst in Europe the two governments remained officially at peace, piracy became the order of the day on the high seas. The most famous pirate was **Sir Francis Drake** who in the **Golden Hind** sailed round the world in **1577-80**. On this voyage he captured the treasure ship **Cacafuego** loaded with 26 tons of silver, 360 000 pieces of eight (gold) and expensive cloth. When Drake got home, the Queen received a 'cut' of the loot and Drake was knighted. When the Spanish Ambassador protested to Elizabeth she denied any knowledge of the event, but it was said at the time that as she was talking to him, the royal dressmaker was measuring her for a new dress in Spanish cloth of gold, stolen on the voyage!

ATTAINMENT TARGET 1: CAUSE, CONSEQUENCE AND CHANGE

1.9

Spain and the Netherlands

Philip II, King of Spain had inherited the Netherlands from his father **Emperor Charles V** in **1555**. The Netherlands, sometimes known as **Flanders**, was wealthy because of the wool trade and cloth making. Flemish merchants had become rich through this trade. Philip II lived in the Netherlands until 1559, when he moved to Spain. Around the same time militant Protestantism was spreading in the Netherlands. A revolt against the rule of Philip II began in **1567**. It was led by **William I (the Silent) Prince of Orange.** William was the great-grandfather of the William of Orange we meet in Unit 4.1.

England and the Netherlands

At first England gave only indirect help to the Netherlands. Elizabeth was anxious to avoid full scale war with Spain. She saw France as a bigger danger to England. However, a Spanish victory in the Netherlands would have threatened England's own cloth trade, as well as removing a potential Protestant ally. In **1584 William the Silent** was assassinated, and in 1585 **Antwerp**, an important port, fell to the Spanish. Elizabeth sent English troops to help the Dutch. Their arrival, in **1586**, helped Philip II make up his mind to invade England.

- Philip II wanted to remove many of the privileges of the 17 provinces of the Netherlands, and govern them directly from **Brussels**.

- Philip wanted to stamp out Protestantism in the Netherlands, and introduced the **Jesuits** and the **Inquisition**. He began burning Protestants at the stake. This also antagonised Flemish Catholics who were tolerant and did not want persecution. In **1566** Protestants rioted, wrecking Catholic churches.

- In 1567 Philip sent a large army to the Netherlands in a show of force, designed to quell opposition. This army began a reign of terror in Flanders.

- The Spanish government imposed heavy taxes on the Netherlands to pay for this army.

Causes of the revolt in the Spanish Netherlands.

A modern replica of Drake's "Golden Hind"

?

1. List all the reasons why Philip II of Spain may have been annoyed with Elizabeth I and England at this time.

2. Which of these reasons do you think is the most important? Give your reasons.

CASE STUDY TWO: THE SPANISH ARMADA

1.10 Philip II

Philip II had been keeping an eye on England for a long time. Spain and England had been allies in the time of **Henry VII** (1485-1509) and **Henry VIII** (1509-1547), but this had weakened with the Protestant Reformation in England in the reign of **Edward VI** (1547-53). However the accession of **Mary 1** (1553-58), a Catholic, returned England to the Spanish camp. Philip II married Mary, and if the marriage had not been childless, England could have become part of the Spanish Empire. Mary's death in **1558** ended any such hopes since her younger sister **Elizabeth I** (1558-1603) was a Protestant. Philip asked Elizabeth to marry him, but she refused.

Philip was convinced that the people of England were Catholic at heart, and he planned to overthrow Elizabeth and replace her with a Catholic monarch-perhaps **Mary Queen of Scots**. The Spanish ambassador to England kept a close eye on the persecution of English Catholics and reported back to Philip regularly as the extracts in Sources A, B, and C show.

A

They [Parliament] have agreed already to a great persecution of the Catholics, who will not attend their churches, and have appointed a commissioner to proceed against them in person and estate.

Spanish Ambassador to Philip II, 18th February 1576.

B

From what I understand, God has been pleased still to maintain some Catholics in this country, and I am told that many persons openly observe the religion, notwithstanding the penalties against it.

Spanish Ambassador to Philip II, 31st March 1578.

C

In accordance with the laws which I said had been passed in this parliament, they have begun to persecute the Catholics worse than ever before, both by condemning them to the £20 fine if they do not attend church every month and by imprisoning them closely in the gaols. The clergymen they succeed in capturing are treated with a variety of terrible tortures: amongst others is one torment that people in Spain imagine to be that which will be worked by Anti-Christ as the most dreadfully cruel of them all. This is to drive iron spikes between the nails and the quick; and two clergymen in the tower have been tortured in this way, one of them being Campion of the Company of Jesus, who, with the other was recently captured. I am assured that when they would not confess under this torture the nails of their fingers and toes were turned back; all of which they suffered with great patience and humility.

Spanish Ambassador to Philip II, 12th August 1581

?

1. What are the strengths and weaknesses of using only the Spanish ambassador's accounts of the treatment of English Catholics? (Sources A, B and C)

2. Why do you think the Pope gave his approval to Philip's plan to attack England?

ATTAINMENT TARGET 2: POINTS OF VIEW

1.10

D

You will cautiously approach His Holiness (the Pope) *and in such terms as you think fit endeavour to obtain from him a secret brief declaring that, failing the Queen of Scotland, The right to the English Crown falls to me ... You will impress upon His Holiness that I cannot undertake a war in England for the purpose merely of placing upon that throne a young heretic like the King of Scotland [James VI] who, indeed, is by his heresy incapacitated to succeed. His Holiness must however be assured that I have no intention of adding England to my own dominions, but to settle the crown upon my daughter, the Infanta.*

Philip II to his Ambassador in Rome, 11th February 1587.

Philip and the Pope

Philip had been pressing the Pope for some time to give his blessing to a Spanish invasion of England. Philip claimed that if Spanish troops landed, thousands of Englishmen would flock to their support. The Pope was not so sure. He was reluctant to offend Philip who was one of the foremost champions of the Catholic faith in Europe, but he suspected that Philip might have other motives, as well as a religious crusade to overthrow Protestantism in England. The Pope did not want the power of Spain to get any greater.

Despite his doubts the Pope eventually felt he had no choice but to approve and bless Philip's invasion plan.

E

Sixteenth century torture

?

3 How does the evidence in Sources C and E illustrate the cruelty which appears to be common in sixteenth century Europe?

4 What sentence in Source D suggests that Philip II is anxious to dispel the Pope's suspicions?

5 Mary, Queen of Scots had been executed on 8th February 1587, three days before Source D was written. What words in the letter suggest that this news had not yet reached Philip?

CASE STUDY TWO: THE SPANISH ARMADA

1.11 The Armada's Voyage

At first Philip planned to send a huge army to England direct from Spain, but this would have required **500 ships** and would have been much too costly. So Philip fell back on a cheaper plan. This plan was to use the Spanish army in the **Netherlands** to invade England. These could be conveyed in flat barges which would be towed across the English channel. They would be protected by a much smaller fleet of warships and supply ships that would sail from Spain to accompany them.

These plans were frustrated by bad luck and by English military action.

> **ACTIVITY**
>
> In groups or with a partner list the advantages and disadvantages of sending an Armada to attack Britain in 1588. What advice would you give Philip II?

A

We whose names are hereunder written, have determined and agreed in council to follow and pursue the Spanish fleet until we have cleared our own coast and brought the firth west of us, and then to return back again as well to restock our ships (which are very short of supplies) as also to guard and defend our own coast at home; with further protestation that, if our lack of food and munitions were supplied, we would pursue them to the furthest they have gone.

The Resolution of the Council of War of the English commanders to fight against the Armada, 1st August 1588

(a) In April **1587** Drake raided **Cadiz** and destroyed 24 big Spanish ships, as well as supply ships. This is sometimes called "singeing the King of Spain's beard".

(b) Several supply ships carrying **barrel staves** (intended for the barrels carrying food for the Armada) were captured. Later the Armada was to suffer from barrels made of unseasoned wood which made the food and water go rotten.

(c) Early in **1588** the commander of the Armada - **Santa Cruz** died. His replacement, chosen for rank rather than experience, was the **Duke of Medina Sidonia** who had little knowledge of the sea.

(d) The Spanish failed to capture a port in the Netherlands with deep enough water to accommodate the Armada.

The Armada Sails

On **20 May 1588** the Armada set sail from Lisbon. It consisted of **130 ships**, drawn from all parts of the Spanish Empire, including rowing galleys from the eastern Mediterranean. The fleet was made up of **75** fighting ships, **25** large merchant ships, and **30** small sloops. They carried 10,000 sailors, 20,000 soldiers and over 2000 artillery pieces. In contrast the English could muster **102** warships, though only 25 were first line ships.

ATTAINMENT TARGET 2: POINTS OF VIEW

1.11

Timeline of the Armada

20 May — Set sail from Lisbon

9 June — Fleet dispersed by storm off **Corunna**. Month's delay to regroup

19 July — English sighted the Armada off Cornwall. **Beacon Fires** relayed the news to Plymouth and London

19-27 July — Nine days battle up the English Channel. The Armada adopted a **crescent formation** with the English attacking from behind

27 July — Spanish fleet anchored off **Calais** hoping for a week to take on fresh supplies.

28 July — Armada attacked in darkness by 8 **Fireships** (Each English commander had given up their oldest ship). In panic many of the Spanish cut their anchors and headed out to sea.

29 July - 3 Aug — Six day battle off the **Kent coast**. Several Spanish ships were sunk. The Spanish could not reach the Netherlands, land in England or regroup. They headed into the **North Sea**. Both sides ran low in ammunition and near the Scottish coast the English turned back.

Aug-Oct — Spanish fleet passes round Scotland and Ireland but is badly damaged by storm and high seas. At least 19 ships are wrecked off the Irish coast. Others are driven out into the Atlantic and founder (sink due to taking in water).

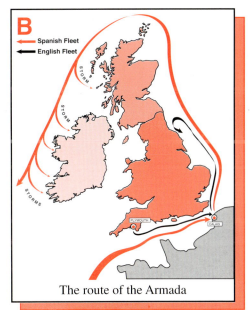

The route of the Armada

About a third of the ships were sunk. Another third were so badly damaged that they could never sail again. **Medina Sidonia** finally got back on **23 October**, delirious from lack of water. A third of the men did not return.

?

1 Put the following reasons for the failure of the Spanish Armada in order of importance.

a) Attack by English fire ships at Calais on July 28th
b) Storms off Ireland and Scotland from August to October
c) Rotten food on board the Spanish ships
d) The death of Santa Cruz, the Spanish Admiral
e) The battle formation of the Spanish fleet
f) Spanish shortage of ammunition
g) The Spanish had poor maps
h) Drake's attack on Cadiz in 1587
i) Failure of the Spanish to get a deep water port in the Netherlands
j) The tactics adopted by the English fleet

2 What would (i) Philip II and (ii) Elizabeth I have regarded as the most important reasons?

CASE STUDY TWO: THE SPANISH ARMADA

1.12 Ireland and the Armada

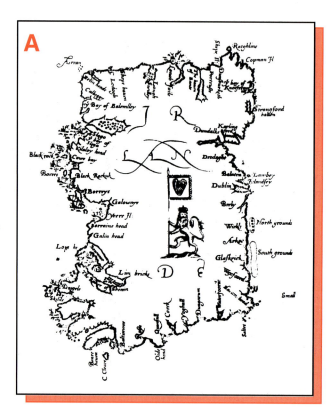

A sixteenth century map of Ireland similar to the maps used by the Spanish.

B Irish Armada Wrecks 1588

Ship	Ton	Soldiers	Sailors	Rowers	Guns	Wrecksite	Date
San Marcos	`790	292	117	0	33	Clare	Sep 20
La Lavia	728	203	71	0	25	Sligo	Sep 25
La Rata Encoronada	820	335	84	0	35	Mayo	Sep 21
La Trinidad Valencera	1100	281	79	0	42	Donegal	Sep 16
La Anunciada	703	196	79	0	24	Clare	Sep 20
San Nicolas Prodaneli	834	274	81	0	26	Mayo	Sep 16
Juliana	860	325	70	0	32	Donegal	?
Santa Maria de Vision	666	236	71	0	18	Sligo	Sep 25
San Juan	530	163	113	0	24	Sligo	Sep 25
La Trinidad	872	180	122	0	24	Kerry	Sep 15
San Juan Batista	652	192	93	0	24	Kerry	Sep 24
Girona	700	169	120	300	50	Antrim	Oct 28
El Gran Grin	1160	256	73	0	28	Clare	Sep 22
U. Duquesa Santa Ana	900	280	77	0	23	Donegal	Sep 26
S. Maria de la Rosa	945	225	64	0	0	Kerry	Sep 21
San Esteban	936	196	68	0	26	Clare	Sep 20
Falcon Blanco Mediano	300	76	27	0	16	Galway	Sep 25
Ciervo Volante	400	200	22	0	18	Mayo	Sep 22
Santiago	600	56	30	0	19	Mayo	Sep 21

ATTAINMENT TARGET 3: USE OF EVIDENCE

1.12

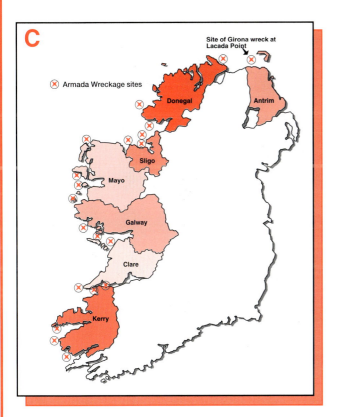

Ireland as it is in reality. The seven counties with Armada wrecks are marked.

Why were so many Spanish ships wrecked off the **west coast of Ireland**? Let us go back to what happened at **Calais**. When the fireships approached the Armada on **28 July**, the Spanish ships had **cut their anchors**. Most ships had at least **one spare** anchor, but if a ship is being carried towards land by an onshore storm, such as the Armada faced off Ireland in September, it will drop anchor to avoid shipwreck. But the ships no longer had enough anchors!

The second factor is that the Spanish thought Ireland look like the map in **Source A**. They assumed that if you sailed round the top of Ireland heading west, you could turn south about ten miles past Donegal. But in reality, if you did that, you would find **Sligo** and **Mayo** in the way! With the wind direction **SW** they could not get back out to sea again. Ten of the nineteen wrecks were off **Mayo**, **Sligo** and **Donegal**. Those Spaniards who did make it ashore, found themselves robbed, stripped, beaten and sometimes killed by the local Irish people.

?

1 A galley was a ship which had oars and rowers. Study Source B. Which Armada wreck was a galley?

2 List the five largest Armada wrecks.

3 In what ways was the information in Source A unreliable?

4 How useful is Source A in helping us to understand why so many Spanish ships were lost around the Spanish coast?

CASE STUDY TWO: THE SPANISH ARMADA

1.12 Ireland and the Armada (continued)

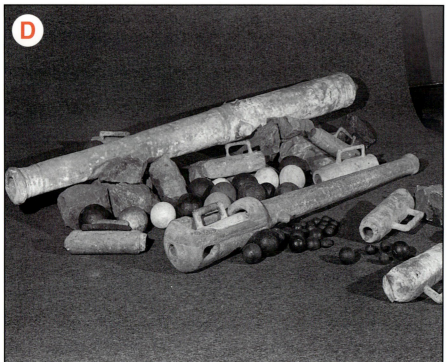

Ordnance from the Girona
The large canon is a bronze half-saker; the smaller one is a bronze esmeril (swivel gun) containing a breech block. Around them are bronze breech blocks and different sizes of stone and iron shot.

The Girona

The most famous Armada wreck was that of the **Girona**. The Girona had managed to find refuge at Killybegs in Donegal, and had been joined there by the crew of two wrecked ships - **Santa Maria Encoronada** and **Duquessa Santa Ana**. The Girona's captain decided to over-winter in Scotland and was heading east along the North Antrim coast when it was wrecked on **28 October** at **Lacada Point** near the Giant's Causeway. Of the 1300 on board 5 survived. In 1967 the wreckage of the Girona was located and divers salvaged hundreds of artifacts including cannon, an anchor, gold chains and jewellery. The ship itself had completely disappeared. The Girona treasure is now in the **Ulster Museum** in Belfast.

> E
>
> *I passed many Spaniards completely naked without any clothes at all, shivering with the cold that was very severe. The night came upon me in this dreary place and I lay down upon some rushes ... a gentleman came up to me, naked, a very gentle youth. He was so frightened that he could not speak, not even to tell me who he was.*

Francisco de Cuellar

ATTAINMENT TARGET 3: USE OF EVIDENCE

1.12

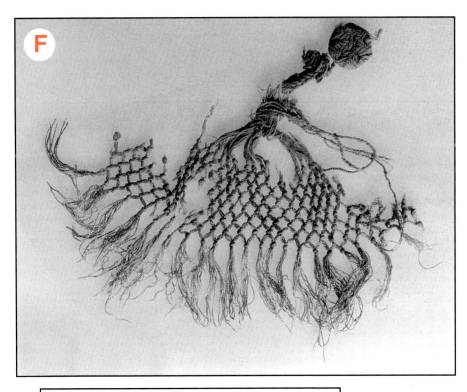

Silk tassle from La Trinidad Valencera.

G

At daybreak I began to go towards a monastery ... but found it torn down, the church and holy images burnt and twelve Spaniards hanged within the church by English Protestants who went about looking for us in order to kill all those who had escaped the hazard of the sea. I found nobody there except the Spaniards dangling from the iron grills in the church windows ... I went out very quickly.

Francisco de Cuellar

The end of the war

The war between England and Spain continued after 1588, but the Armada was its climax. In **1598** Philip II died and in **1603** Elizabeth I. Her successor, James I made peace with Spain in **1604**.

?

5 Sources E and G were written by a Spaniard therefore they must be unreliable. Explain why you agree or disagree with this.

6 How useful is it for an historian to have pictures of the wrecked ship Girona and its contents?

THE EXPERIENCE OF COLONISATION AND PLANTATION

2.1 What is a Colony?

A good definition of a colony is:

> a settlement in a new country, forming a community which is either partly or fully subject to the mother state.

In the 15th and 16th centuries, many European countries established colonies in various parts of the world, especially in those areas which are now known as the Americas. Soon these Spanish and Portuguese explorers were followed by **Conquistadors** (Conquerors). They discovered ancient but advanced civilisations such as the **Aztecs** of Mexico and the **Incas** of Peru. These colonies in South America had huge quantities of gold and silver which were sent back to Europe in treasure ships.

B

If our nation were once planted in North America, or near thereabouts; whereas [English fishing boats] now fish but for two months of the year, they might then fish for so long as pleased themselves.

Hakluyt: *Principal Navigations* Vol VIII, 1598-1600

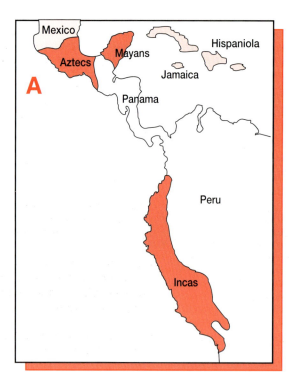

Map of Central America, showing the location of the Inca and Aztec civilisations.

C

... it is well known that all savages ... as soon as they shall begin but a little to taste of civility, will take marvellous delight in any garment, be it never so simple; as a shirt, a blue, yellow, red or green cotton cassock, a cap, or such like, and will take incredible pains for such a trifle ... how great benefit to all Clothiers, Woolmen, Carders, Spinners, Weavers, Fullers etc would be the establishment of colonies in America and Far East.

Hakluyt: *Principal Navigations* Vol VIII, 1598-1600

ATTAINMENT TARGET 3: USE OF EVIDENCE

2.1

D

... this voyage is not altogether undertaken for ourselves but ... the Savages shall have cause to bless the hour when this enterprise was undertaken.

First and chiefly, in respect of the most happy and gladsome tidings of the most glorious gospel of our Saviour, Jesus Christ, whereby they may be brought from falsehood to truth ...

...being brought from brutish ignorance to civility and knowledge, they may be taught how one tenth of their land, if manured and ploughed, would yield as much as the whole presently does...But this is not all the benefit they shall receive: for over and beside the knowledge how to till and dress their grounds, they shall be reduced from unseemly customs to honest manners, from disordered riotous routs to a well governed Commonwealth ...

Hakluyt: *Principal Navigations* Vol VIII, 1598-1600

E

It will prove a general benefit unto our country that, not only a great number of men which do now live idly at home and are a burden, chargeable and unprofitable to this realm, shall hereby be set to work, but also children of twelve and fourteen years of age or older, may be kept from idleness, in making of a thousand kinds of trifling things which will be good merchandize for that country and, moreover, our idle women shall also be employed in plucking, drying and sorting of feathers, in pulling, beating and working of hemp, and in gathering of cotton, and diverse things for dyeing.

Hakluyt: *Principal Navigations* Vol VIII, 1598-1600

Many English people believed that they too should seek colonies in North America.

Study sources B, C, D and E and answer the questions below.

?

1. What do Sources B, C, D and E tell you about the English view of the natives of North America?

2. Which source would most appeal to an English wool merchant? Give reasons for your answer.

3. To which group would Source C be addressed?

4. List the reasons given in all four sources for England to have colonies in North America.

5. List these reasons in rank order from the point of view of (a) a merchant/trader and (b) an Anglican bishop.

6. Suggest reasons why the rank orders may differ from each other.

7. Sources B, C, D and E came from the same book. What does this tell us about its author, Hakluyt?

THE EXPERIENCE OF COLONISATION AND PLANTATION

2.2　Colonies and Trade

Trading links were important reasons for setting up colonies abroad (See Sources A and B). Improved navigation techniques meant that much longer voyages could be undertaken by adventurous sailors. New areas were conquered all over the known world and, of course, each new area had something valuable to be exploited by the European countries. Some of these goods were spices to enhance food and cooking. Others included tobacco and dyes but the sixteenth century also saw the beginning of a slave trade. This normally took the form of capturing natives on the West coast of Africa and taking them to America where they were sold as slaves.

During this period some trade journeys were made partially overland, such as the silk route to and from China and cottons from India.

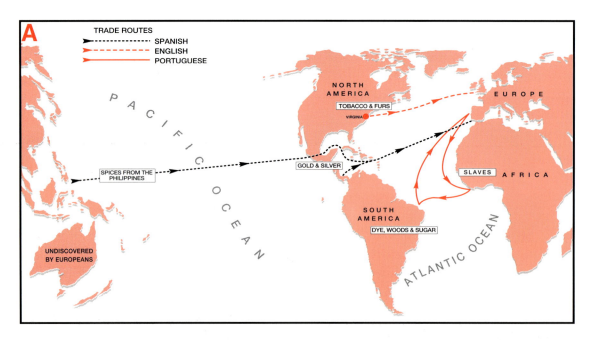

Sixteenth century trade between Europe, Africa and the Americas.

ATTAINMENT TARGET 3: USE OF EVIDENCE

2.2

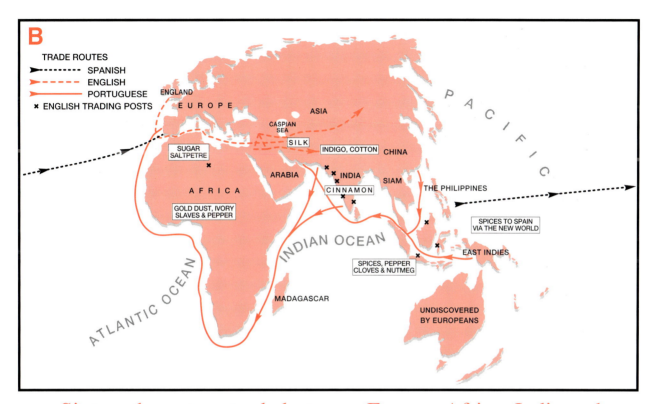

Sixteenth century trade between Europe, Africa, India and the Far East during Elizabeth's reign.

?

1. Using Source A, list the goods received by England, Spain and Portugal from the Americas.

2. Which country do you think would become richest from this trade alone, and why do you think this is the case?

3. Study the English trade routes in Source B. Suggest ways in which English goods were transported from India to England.

4. What problems may these routes have caused?

5. "Any historical source is useful to an historian". Do you agree? Refer to these maps in your answer.

6. What additional evidence would be needed to give a fuller picture of the trading links between the colonies and Europe in the sixteenth century?

THE EXPERIENCE OF COLONISATION AND PLANTATION

2.3 The American Colonies

In 1606, the English King, James I, granted permission to the London Virginia Company to take control of a large area of land in Virginia. They hoped to discover gold and silver there. This colony was called **Jamestown**. One of the pioneers was called **John Smith**. The colonists sailed in 3 ships - Discovery, Susan Constant, and God Speed. They reached Chesapeake Bay in April 1607 and saw "fair meadows, and goodley trees, with fresh waters."

The Indians were friendly at first. The first thing the new settlers did was to chose a site and the London Company had given specific instructions about this. **Jamestown**, which the colonists built, did not fulfil all the requirements but was the best site they could find. They built a fort there so that they would be safe if attacked. The next urgent tasks were to clear the ground, to make temporary houses for themselves, to plant vegetables, and to make nets for catching their food. They also had to start filling the ships with a cargo to take home, because the London Company wanted its profit.

A

There were never Englishmen left in a foreign country in such misery as we were in this new discovered Virginia. We watched every three nights, lying on the bare cold ground, what weather so ever came; warded [guarded] all the next day; which brought our men to be most feeble wretches, not having five able men to man our bulwarks [strong defences] upon any occasion.

From *Captain John Smith and Virginia* (Then and There Series, Longman 1968)

B

Pocahontas, the King's dearest daughter, when no entreaty could prevail, got his head in her armes, and laid her owne upon his to save him from death: whereat the King was contented he should live to make him hatchets, and her bells, beads and copper; for they thought him as well of all other occupations as themselves, for the King himselfe will make his own robes, shooes, bowes, arrowes, pots.

From *Captain John Smith and Virginia* (Then and There Series, Longman 1968)

John Smith

Before leaving England, the names of those chosen by the London Virginia Company to govern the Colony were put in a locked box. This was opened when they reached America, and one of the seven names was **John Smith** who was an army captain. However, he had quarrelled so much with the others that he was not made a council member. Later (in May) the native Indian people became unfriendly and raided the colony so Smith was asked to help the colonists defend Jamestown.

?
List the various problems which faced these early settlers.

Smith believed that the colonists needed to be made to work. He said, "If you do not work, you shall not eat". He took command. See Source C.

By September 1607 half of the original 104 settlers were dead from malaria or typhoid. As those who survived were very weak, it was even more necessary to build defences. (See Source A)

36

ATTAINMENT TARGET 2: POINTS OF VIEW

2.3

Pocahontas

The most pressing problem was shortage of food. Until they could grow their own crops, they had to trade with the Indians. They gave the Indians beads, copper and hatchets in return for bread, venison, turkeys and wild fowl. On one of these expeditions Smith was captured by some Indians who were going to kill him by beating his brains out. What happened next is related in Source B.

Smith returned to his colony and was made President on 10 September **1608**. He extended the fort, tightened the discipline of the colonists and trained military units. The cargo was still being sent to England where merchants were looking for pitch, tar, soap-ashes and cut wood. Smith was bitter, because these things were not abundant in Virginia where the colonists were struggling to live. Colonists now were very disgruntled, but Smith kept them together, mainly because they were impressed by his exploits.

C

... by his own example, good words, and fair promises set some to mow, others to bind thatch; some to build houses, others to thatch them; himself always bearing the greatest task for his own share; so that, in short time, he provided most of them lodgings, neglecting any for himself.

From *Captain John Smith and Virginia* (Then and There Series, Longman 1968)

Smith leaves Virginia

In July **1609** a ship left England carrying vital supplies, but also letters criticising Smith for not sending back enough goods. Some great men in England decided to govern Virginia, and Smith returned to London.

The colony grew gradually, but Indian massacres in 1622 and 1644 affected the flow of settlers. Eventually, the Indians were defeated by the better weapons of the colonists. A new town was built further inland, away from the unhealthy swamps, and great plantations developed using negro slaves.

Pocahontas saving John Smith's life in 1607.

ACTIVITY

When John Smith returned to London, people in Virginia were left with mixed feelings about him. Form groups. Half of the groups prepare speeches defending the actions of John Smith; the other half condemning him. Representatives of these groups may present their evidence to a tribunal which, on the basis of this evidence, decides John Smith's fate.

THE EXPERIENCE OF COLONISATION AND *P*LANTATION

2.4 Ireland before the Plantations

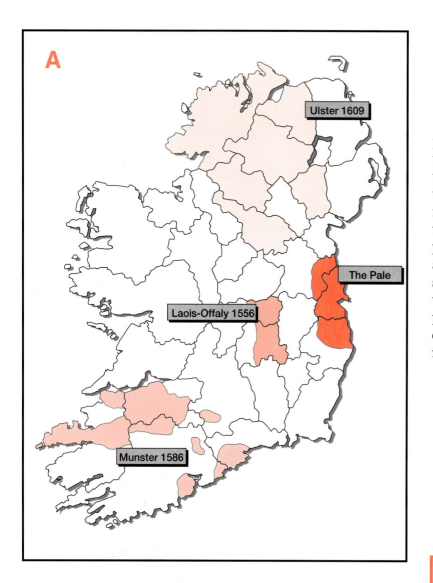

Early Plantations in Ireland

The English faced many problems in Ireland, but from the middle of the 16th century they had gradually extended their control over Ireland. One method which they used was the establishment of **plantations**, where English and Scottish planters or settlers had come to live and work in Ireland. Early plantation schemes were carried out in Laois, Offaly and in Munster.

ACTIVITY

Form groups. You will compose a speech to be delivered to the English parliament in 1608. Half of the groups state the benefits of Plantation in Ireland. The other half express objections.

ATTAINMENT TARGET 1: CAUSE, CONSEQUENCE AND CHANGE

2.4

The Pale is a district around Dublin and is the only area ruled directly by us. Dublin is the centre of English rule in Ireland.

A barbarous country must first be broken by war before it will be capable of good government.

We see Spain as a dangerous neighbour.

The Irish chiefs looked to Spain for help during the Desmond rebellion in Munster.

The Irish remain Catholic, Gaelic and use their own laws.

Our Protestant King, Henry VIII, took the title "King of Ireland". Tudor governments try to make all Ireland obey English law.

?

1. Which of the reasons for Plantation support these statements:
   (a) England was worried about foreign enemies
   (b) Religious differences were seen as a problem
   (c) England wished to extend control over Ireland?

2. Which of these reasons do *you* think was the most important? Give reasons for your answer.

THE EXPERIENCE OF COLONISATION AND *P*LANTATION

2.5 Plantation

The Nine Years' War

After 1594 some of the most important Irish clans had gone to war against the forces of **Queen Elizabeth**. They were led by **Hugh O'Neill** who was also known as the **Earl of Tyrone**.

The Irish claimed that they were fighting to preserve their old way of life which was being threatened by English rule. This old way of life meant the Irish system of laws and the Roman Catholic faith. For some years they were successful, but on **24 December 1601** Irish forces were defeated at the **Battle of Kinsale**. Although O'Neill came back to Tyrone with his army, he knew that he had little chance of success against the English.

During 1602 the English strengthened their forts around O'Neill's territory in Tyrone. Lord Mountjoy ordered crops and cattle to be destroyed so the Irish would be starved into submission.

The Treaty of Mellifont

In the same year, one of O'Neill's allies, the head of the O'Cahan clan, made peace with the English. O'Neill still refused to surrender. The English decided to make peace as the war had proved very costly. So the **Treaty of Mellifont** was signed in **1603**. O'Neill gave up his Irish title and accepted English laws. In return he was allowed to keep his lands.

Many of the English who had fought in Ulster saw how prosperous a land it could be and they were prepared to take a chance to live there.

A

A Replica Plantation House

Ulster History Park, Omagh, Co. Tyrone

B

Edmund Spenser, Description of Munster, 1580

Sure it is a most beautiful sweet country as any under heaven ... adorned with goodly woods fit for building houses and ships, full of good ports and havens ... beside the soil itself is most fertile fit to yield all kinds of fruit ... and lastly the heaven most mild and temperate.

ACTIVITY

Rank order the reasons for supporting a plantation in Ulster from the point of view of an Englishman.

ATTAINMENT TARGET 2: POINTS OF VIEW

2.5

C

Art thou a tradesman, a smith, a weaver? Go to Ireland. Thou shall be higher in estimation and quickly enriched.

Art thou a [farmer] whose worth is not past ten or twenty pounds? Go thither. Thou shall whistle sweetly and feed thy whole family if they be six, for sixpence a day.

Art thou a minister of God's word? Make speed ... Thou shalt there see the poor ignorant untaught people worship stones and sticks. Thou, by carrying millions to heaven, may be made an Archangel.

From *A Direction for the Plantation in Ulster* by Thomas Blenerhasset, Fermanagh, 1610

The English Government's problem was that Spain could join with the Irish and use Ireland as a base from which they could attack England. Officials in London believed that as long as Catholics held land, they could raise the men and equipment necessary to stage a rebellion. Consequently, the English decided to plant colonies with loyal Protestants, giving them land and support in order that they could survive. Before the plan for Ulster, plantations had been carried out in : **Laois-Offaly (1556); Ards in Co Down (1570); Antrim (1573).**

English Expectations of Plantation

(a) Ports would develop as trade expands.

(b) New towns would grow at Cookstown, Strabane, Letterkenny, Londonderry and Coleraine.

(c) English and Scottish planters would move in.

(d) Catholic populations would be driven to poor land in the west of the country. Former landowners would now become tenants or labourers.

(e) English soldiers and government officials could buy cheap land in Ireland.

(f) Hopefully, a plantation of English and Loyal Irish would end threats of rebellion.

D

1 *The securing of that wilde Countrye to the Crowne of England.*

2 *The withdrawing of all the charge of the Garrison and men in warre.*

3 *The rewarding of the olde servitors to their good content.*

4 *The meanes how to increase the revenue to the Crowne with a yearly very great somme.*

5 *How to establish the Purite of Religion there.*

6 *And how the undertakers may with securite be inriched.*

Principal aims of the Plantation given in *A Direction for the Plantation in Ulster* by Thomas Blenerhasset

?

1 What kind of settlers would Source C attract to come to Ulster?

2 How can you tell from their expectations that the English government had high hopes for the success of the plantation scheme? (See left)

THE EXPERIENCE OF COLONISATION AND Plantation

2.6 The Ulster Plantation

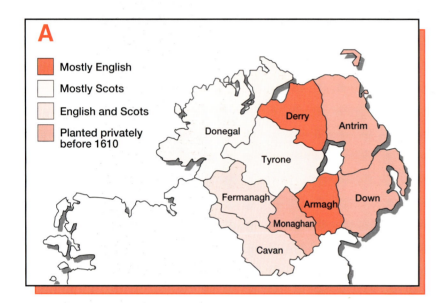

The Province of Ulster, showing the counties planted in 1610

ACTIVITY

If you are familiar with Londonderry or another plantation town as it is today, see if you can trace the town centre and the road or street patterns.

After the defeat of O'Neill in Ulster, O'Neill and some other northern chiefs fled from Lough Swilly in **1607** in what has become known as the **Flight of the Earls**. The Irish Lord Deputy, **Sir Arthur Chichester**, was convinced that the only way to control Ulster was to plant it with English and Scottish settlers. Chichester himself colonised land around Belfast where a street is named after him.

In 1609 a number of commissioners travelled the area, mapping the land and finding out who the owners were. They also decided which land belonged to the Church of Ireland, because it was not to be confiscated. As some people could not prove their ownership of land, it was usually taken from them.

About 4 million acres were involved in the scheme, but much of this was not very good land. Some lessons had been learned from earlier plantations. Settlers were not to live in scattered houses, but in fortified villages and towns.

?

1. What does Source B (Map of Derry) tell us about the town planning of these settlers?

2. What other evidence would you need to have if you wished to prove that all the plantation towns followed this pattern?

ATTAINMENT TARGET 3: USE OF EVIDENCE

2.6

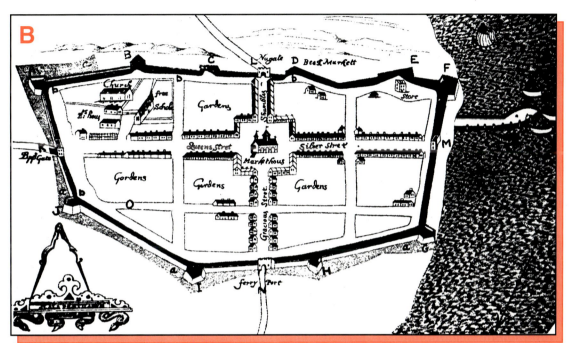

Map of Derry in 1625.

Land was granted to:

1 English and Scottish Undertakers

These people undertook to settle their estates with English and Scottish tenants only. If they got 1,000 acres, they were to build a fortified enclosure called a bawn. If they got 1,500 or 2,000 acres, they had to build a castle as well. Tenants were to live near the bawn and keep arms ready in case of attack.

2 Servitors

These people had served the crown in Ireland and were allowed to have Irish tenants. They had to take the same defensive precautions as the undertakers.

3 Loyal Irish

About one tenth of the land was given to Irishmen whom the government trusted. They were to build and settle their estates in the same way as servitors, and use English farming methods.

4 Guilds

The London Guilds, which had already been involved in the plantation of Virginia, were keen to be part of the Ulster plantation too. King James, recognising that these guilds were wealthy, was attracted by their interest and they were given Co Derry. These guilds formed the Irish Society to look after their interests. It was this connection with London which led to the change of name to Co Londonderry. They were often absentee landowners, but they did much to shape that county, including the building of towns in the English Style.

5 Others

The rest of the land was given to the established church, Trinity College and six free schools. A number of new towns were also built.

THE EXPERIENCE OF COLONISATION AND *P*LANTATION

2.6 The Ulster Plantation (continued)

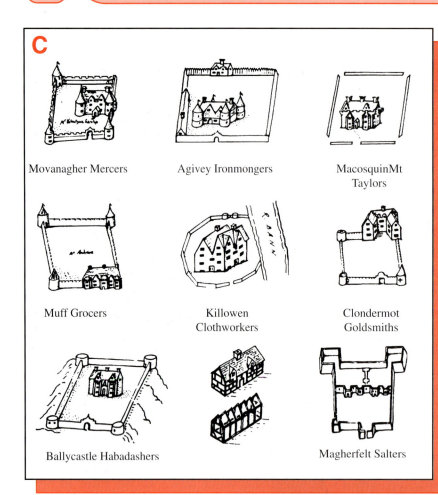

Above: Examples of Plantation Bawns.

?

3 What do the bawns in Source C have in common and how do they differ?

4 Find the meaning of
    (a) mercer
    (b) habadasher
    (c) salter

5 What do the names in Question 4 and the other names in Source C suggest about the people who built these bawns?

Right: Interior of replica plantation bawn at the Ulster History Park, Omagh, Co. Tyrone.

ATTAINMENT TARGETS 1 AND 3

2.6

ACTIVITY

Study the picture of Monea Castle as it is today, (Source F), and the artist's impression in Source E. Can you match up the present day remains with the artist's drawing? How could you check the accuracy of his drawing?

Right: An artist's impression of Monea Castle, Co Fermanagh.

Below: Monea Castle as it is today.

45

THE EXPERIENCE OF COLONISATION AND PLANTATION CASE STUDY

2.7 OMAGH — a Plantation Case Study

A

Round this place there is great desolation, by reason of which it happeneth that merchants and other passengers weekly guarded travelling from Derrie or Liffer to the Pale are usually in their passage cut off and murdered.

Sir Arthur Chichester's description of Omagh.

In **1602** O'Neill was defeated by **Lord Mountjoy** at Omagh as the Nine Years' War drew to a close. You can read what Sir Arthur Chichester said about the town in Source A.

In 1609 the town and district were granted to **Lord Castlehaven**, who failed to erect a castle and settle the proper number of English on the land. As a result, these lands reverted to the crown and were then granted to Captain Edmund Leigh and his brothers John and Daniel.

This was not the only place where Lord Castlehaven had not fulfilled his undertaking. Source B is a description of Lord Castlehaven's estate at Forkhill, Co Armagh.

By 1611 Omagh seemed to be well improved. Read Source C.

Later in 1631, Charles I granted the manor of Arleston or Audleston, of 2000 acres of land in and around Omagh to James Mervyn. Mervyn built three castles. There is now no trace of the castle at Ballynahatty. Of the other two, only the corners remain standing at Trillick and at Kirlish, near Drumquin.

B

The Earl of Castlehaven hath 3,000 acres. Upon this there is no building at all, either of Bawns or Castle ...I find planted on this land some few English families ...(who) since the old Earl died, (as they tell me) cannot have (land) unless, they will bring treble the rent which they paid; and yet they ... have but half the land which they enjoyed in the old Earl's time...

The Earl hath more 2,000 acres... Upon this there was a large house begun, but it is pulled down and made but half so great ... The Agent for the Earl showed me the Rent-Roll of all the Tenants ... but they are all leaving the land. The rest of the land is let to twenty Irish gentlemen ... and these Irish Gentlemen have under them about 3,000 souls of all sorts.

Above: A description of Lord Castlehaven's estate at Forkhill, Co. Armagh. From Pynnar's *Survey* 1619

C

The Fort of Omye. Here is a good fort fairly walled with lime and stone about thirty feet high above the ground with a parapet, the river on one side and a large deep ditch about the rest; in which is built a fair house of timber after the English manner. Begun by Captain Edmund Leigh and finished by his brothers, at their own change, upon the lands of the Abbey of Omye, at which place are many families of English and Irish, who have built them good dwelling houses, which is a safety and comfort for passengers between Dungannon and Liffer. The fort is a place of good import upon all occasions of service and fit to be maintained.

Left: Lord Carew, writing in 1611.

ATTAINMENT TARGET 3: USE OF EVIDENCE

2.7

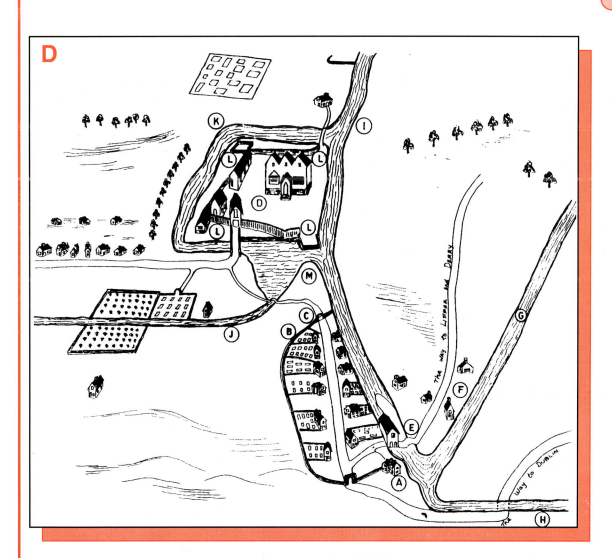

D

The earliest map of Omagh, 1610

KEY

A = Old Castle
(Dublin Road Corner)
B = A Cross
C = Northern Gate
D = Bawn
E = Mill
F = Inn for Travellers
G = Camowen River
H = Drumragh River
I = Strule River
J = Brook
K = Moat
L = Gun emplacements
M = Gates to the Basin

1 These sources are all primary evidence. How are they useful to an historian studying the beginnings of a plantation town?

2 In what ways is the bawn at Omagh similar to the other examples of bawns which you have seen in Unit 2.6?

3 Who may have drawn the map of Omagh and for what reason?

47

THE EXPERIENCE OF COLONISATION AND PLANTATION

2.8 The Results of the Ulster Plantation

A

When the Galloway planters came to Ulster they were only returning to their own lands like emigrants returning home again.

F.J. Biggar, quoted by I. Adamson in *The Identity of Ulster*, Pretani Press, 1982

The colonists were always in danger from the native Irish, mainly from the swordsmen who were the armed followers of the dispossessed chiefs. The government even shipped some of them to the continent, but most of them escaped and lived rough in the woods and hills. These people were called **woodkern**. Look at Source D.

They tried to stop the planters from building and often attacked their farms. This was one of the main reasons why it was so difficult to get English and Scottish tenants to settle on the land.

Scots had settled in Ulster before the plantation, mainly in Antrim and Down where **Hugh Montgomery** and **James Hamilton** from Ayrshire had settled. They were very successful, perhaps because they were not regarded as strangers by the Irish.

The Scots came in large numbers and helped contribute to the success of the plantation, even though they were not part of the government's original scheme.

They also brought their **Presbyterian** religion with them. The Presbyterian church permitted ordinary members to play an important part in governing their church.

However, not all Scots were regarded as a good influence as Sources B and C show.

But not all planters were Protestant. The Bishop of Derry wrote to The Lord Chancellor in 1629: " Sir George Hamilton ... has done his best to plant Popery ..., and brought over priests ... from Scotland..."

B

From Scotland came many and from England not a few, yet all of them generally the scum of both nations who from debt or law breaking and fleeing from justice come hither ... most of these people ... cared little for any church ... with fighting, murder, adultery, etc.

From *History of the Church of Ireland after the Scots were Naturalised*, 1670-71, by Andrew Stewart; edited by W.D. Killen, Belfast, 1866

C

... the most part were such as either poverty, scandalous lives, or at the best adventurers seeking of better accommodation had forced thither ... the security and thriving of religion was little seen to by these adventurers and the preachers were generally ... the same.

From *The Life of Mr. Robert Blair*, about 1663 by R. Blair; edited by T. McCrie, Edinburgh, 1848.

ACTIVITY

Use the library to find out origins of the surnames of the people in your class. Use this information to construct a chart or pie graph showing who has English, Scottish, Irish or other roots

ATTAINMENT TARGET 2: POINTS OF VIEW

2.8

Woodkern on a raid

As a result of the plantation, a different way of life from the rest of Ireland was brought to Ulster by the colonists. Not only did the Scots bring their religious beliefs, but they also brought modern farming methods and a tradition of the Puritan work ethic. This did much to make North East Ulster different from the rest of Ireland.

However, the native Irish were never fully removed from the land and purely British settlements were not established. The rebellion of **1641** shows that the ability of the native Irish in Ulster to wage war was not destroyed by the plantation process, even though it was by then too firmly established to be overthrown.

?

While some people gained much as a result of the Plantation, others were not so pleased. How did (a) Irish Catholics who had lost land, and (b) Irish Protestant landowners who had felt threatened by O'Neill, react to the Plantation?
Try to explain why they felt as they did. If possible support your ideas with relevant sources.

POLITICAL AND RELIGIOUS CONFLICT IN BRITAIN

3.1 James I and the Puritans

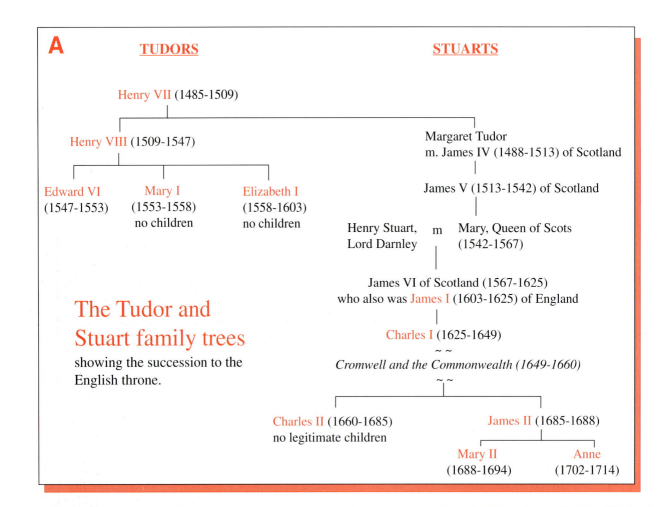

A — The Tudor and Stuart family trees showing the succession to the English throne.

Queen Elizabeth died in 1603, and as she had no children, this brought to an end the period of Tudor rule. The new king was **James I (1603-25)** whose mother, Mary Queen of Scots, had been executed by Elizabeth in 1587. James I was succeeded by his son, **Charles I (1625-49)**, but his reign ended with his execution following the **Civil War**. From 1649-1660 England was without a king, and during this period of the **Commonwealth**, which meant a free state without a monarch, the leading figure was **Oliver Cromwell**. In 1660 the monarchy was restored as **Charles II (1660-85)** returned to England to become king.

?

1. From the point of view of (a) a Puritan and (b) a Roman Catholic, write two letters to James I in 1604, asking him to look favourably on your religion. Mention his background and why, because of this, you think he should favour your cause.

2. Suggest reasons why these letters would differ.

James I.

James was married to Anne of Denmark. They had seven children of whom only three survived childhood.

James believed very strongly in the Divine Right of Kings. This meant that he believed absolutely that he had been chosen by God to be King and therefore ordinary people should not question what he said and did.

He disliked the habit of tobacco smoking very much and wrote a pamphlet in 1604 entitled "Counterblasts to Tobacco", condemning this habit.

James also had many concerns about religion in general. He commissioned an Authorised Version of the Bible in English. This version, sometimes still called the King James Version, came out in 1611.

He was also interested in converting the Psalms into metrical form so that they could be sung. He was doing this himself but died before they were published in 1631.

The main religious problems in the British Isles at this time.

Both James I and Charles I faced opposition from various religious groups. The three main religious groups active at this time were:-

Anglicans: The Anglican way of worship and the rule of bishops had become common during Elizabeth's reign and the majority of the population wanted this to continue. James himself favoured the Anglicans and this angered the other two religious groups. The leading figure in the Anglican church was **Archbishop Laud** who was bitterly opposed to Puritans.

James VI of Scotland and I of England

Puritans: The Puritans were more extreme Protestants who favoured simple church services and a "religious" lifestyle - the Puritan way of life. As James had been brought up by Puritan nobles in Scotland, the Puritans hoped for favours from the new king. James met the Puritans in 1604 at the Hampton Court Conference. When James I did not favour them, they were angry and a small group left England to found a new state in America. They were known as the **Pilgrim Fathers** and they sailed to America on the **Mayflower** in **1620**.

Catholics: The Catholics also hoped for favours from James, and although both his mother and his wife were Catholic, James I ignored their demands once he became king in 1603. As a result, a small number of Catholic nobles began plotting against the king, and this led to the **Gunpowder Plot** of 1605.

POLITICAL AND RELIGIOUS CONFLICT IN BRITAIN

3.2 The Gunpowder Plot

Guy Fawkes and other conspirators in the Gunpowder Plot.

Soon after James became king in 1603 it became clear to leading Catholics in England that they could not expect protection from the new ruler. Therefore, they decided to take over the government of England by killing the king and the most important men in the country, when they were together at the state opening of Parliament. Their plan was to blow up Parliament on the **5 November 1605**, and put a new Catholic king on the throne. The plotters had rented a cellar beneath the Houses of Parliament and when the plot was discovered, a total of 36 barrels of gunpowder was found hidden under a pile of firewood. A trail of gunpowder was laid from the barrels to the door. When it was ignited, the plotters reckoned that it would burn slowly for fifteen minutes before setting off the barrels in a massive explosion.

ACTIVITY

Find out how the Gunpowder Plot is remembered today

ATTAINMENT TARGET 3: USE OF EVIDENCE

3.2

B

My lord - out of the love I bear to some of your friends, I have a care of your preservation. Therefore I warn you ... to devise some excuse to shift your attendance at this Parliament ... They shall receive a terrible blow this Parliament and yet they shall not see who hurts them ... The danger is past as soon as you have burnt this letter.

An extract from the Monteagle letter.

A cartoon drawn in 1617 showing the Monteagle letter being delivered just in time to save the King.

The Monteagle Letter

The plot failed because one of the plotters, **Francis Tresham**, tried to warn his brother-in-law, **Lord Monteagle**, to stay away from the state opening of Parliament. Tresham sent a very mysterious letter to Monteagle and it was shown to James I (see Source B). The letter raised the King's suspicions and he ordered a search of the cellars of the House of Lords on the 4 November. This led to the arrest of **Guy Fawkes** and after being tortured in the Tower of London, he confessed his role in the Gunpowder Plot.

Lord Monteagle's family was Catholic and he had been involved in a rebellion in 1601 against Queen Elizabeth I. He was released from prison after paying a heavy fine. In 1603 he supported King James, and in 1605 he wrote to the King saying he had become a Protestant (see Source D). Lord Monteagle was even allowed to sit in the House of Lords.

D

I will live and die in that religion which I have now resolved to profess.

Lord Monteagle in 1605

1. Why do you think Tresham sent the letter (Source B) to Monteagle?

2. How might Monteagle's comments about his religion (Source D) have influenced his decision to show the letter to the King?

3. Source C is a cartoon. Is such a source reliable as evidence?

53

POLITICAL AND RELIGIOUS CONFLICT IN BRITAIN

3.3 Charles I and Parliament

The first half of the seventeenth century was dominated by a struggle for **political** power between the Stuart Kings and Parliament. Conflict arose, because the King and Parliament had different ideas about who should exercise most power in the country. In those days, Parliament met very infrequently and usually only when a decision had to be made about raising money through taxes to pay for wars or other major crises. Then, monarchs could go to Parliament and actually become involved directly in law making. Many MPs wanted Parliament to have more power. In the first half of the seventeenth century most MPs were wealthy landowners.

The great issue in this quarrel between King and Parliament was **money**. The King needed money to run the country, but it was Parliament which raised this money by controlling taxes. A head-on clash was bound to happen sooner or later, but it did not occur during James's reign. When Parliament refused to give money, James dismissed the MPs, but they did not want to challenge the King in an open contest.

During the reign of Charles I the conflict between King and Parliament worsened. In particular, Charles found himself quarrelling with **Puritan MPs**, and in 1629 he dismissed Parliament and ruled for eleven years on his own. Of course, the King had to continue to collect taxes, and

A

Charles I attempting to arrest five Members of Parliament.

this gradually turned ordinary people against Charles. Indeed many observers believed that the King's unpopular taxes were illegal, and by 1640 he was forced to recall Parliament as he was desperately short of money.

Therefore, one major cause of the English Civil War, which brought the reign of Charles I to an end, was **money**. This had caused most of the quarrelling between King and Parliament. Another major cause was **religion**. Most Puritans wanted bishops to be dismissed and the English prayer book (Anglican) abolished.

ATTAINMENT TARGET 1: CAUSE, CONSEQUENCE AND CHANGE

3.3

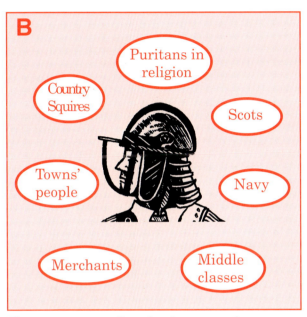

These were groups of people who supported Parliament in the Civil War.

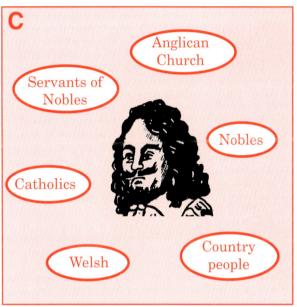

These were groups of people who supported the King in the Civil War

What was the English Civil War?

In 1642 the quarrel between the King and Parliament broke into open conflict (fighting). Charles had tried to impose his authority by arresting five MPs who had been especially active against him (see Source A). However, the five escaped by boat down the River Thames to the City of London, and when the King and a troop of soldiers tried to follow them, they were chased out of the city by angry groups of citizens. Civil war was guaranteed.

For the English Civil War, like other civil wars, it is difficult to define clearly who supported each side. For example, one village may have supported the King, while the neighbouring village may have sided with Parliament. As a general guide, however, the diagrams above give some indication of which groups supported King and Parliament.

ACTIVITY

Divide your page into two columns. List the groups which supported Parliament on one side and those who supported the King on the other. In each case, suggest why they were on one side or the other.

?

Explain what were the main causes of the argument between King and Parliament

POLITICAL AND RELIGIOUS  CONFLICT IN BRITAIN

3.4 The English Civil War

Time Line of the English Civil War

1642	22 August	War declared.
	23 October	Battle of Edgehill - Royalist victory.
	13 Nov	King retreats to H.Q. in Oxford.
1643	Jan-May	Royalists do well in North, East, Midlands, Wales and Borders, and the West. Parliament does well in South and Central England.
	20 Sept	Indecisive First Battle of Newbury.
	25 Sept.	20,000 Scottish troops come to help Parliament.
1644	19 January	Scottish army enters England.
	Jan-March	Royalist defeats in N. Midlands and South.
	2 July	Cromwell wins at Marston Moor.
	27 October	Inconclusive Second Battle of Newbury.
1645	February	Unsuccessful peace negotiations.
	April	New Model Army created.
	14 June	Battle of Naseby.
	June - Sept.	New Model Army has several victories.
1646	5 May	King surrenders to Scots and is taken to Newcastle.
	13 July	Peace terms presented to the King.
1647	March	Scottish army goes home.
	May	Short of money, parliament pays off most of the New Model Army
	June	Army refuses to retire until properly paid and a fair settlement reached with the King.
	1 August	Army puts forward its own peace terms.
	26 December	King persuades Scots to join his side and invade England.
1648	March-May	Royalists defeated by New Model Army in South East and Wales.
	2 August	Scots defeated at Preston.
	6 December	Army officers take over Parliament.
1649	20 January	This new Parliament puts the King on trial.
	27 January	Death sentence declared on the King.
	30 January	Charles I executed.
	February	House of Lords and Monarchy abolished.

Suggest why Parliament's side won the Civil War.

A Cavalier, who supported the King.

ACTIVITY

In groups, compose speeches to be delivered to their respective armies by the King and by Oliver Cromwell.
Explain in these why you are fighting and why victory is essential to your side.

ATTAINMENT TARGET 1: CAUSE CONSEQUENCE AND CHANGE

3.4

When the civil war began in 1642 the King's supporters (Cavaliers) and Parliament's supporters (Roundheads) were evenly matched.

From the outset, however, the King appeared to have an advantage, because the nobles who supported him were skilled horsemen, but this was more than wiped out by the formation of the **New Model Army** at the end of **1644**. This new army quickly proved itself to be a very professional and efficient force which would guarantee Parliament's success in the civil war. In **1646** the King surrendered, and the New Model Army offered to let Charles remain King if he would agree to let everyone **except Catholics** worship as they pleased. The King was a proud man and as he did not want either Parliament or the army to dictate terms to him, he began plotting against Parliament. This resulted in the re-opening of the civil war in **1648**, but again Charles was decisively beaten. Naturally, the army generals were furious at the King's attempts to deceive them, and although many MPs in Parliament urged caution, the army was determined to execute Charles.

Charles I was executed in 1649, and from 1649 to 1660 England was without a king.

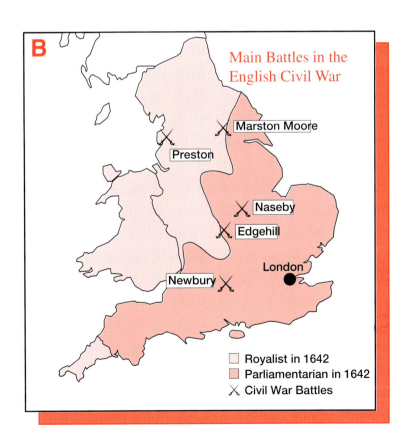

A Roundhead, who supported Parliament.

POLITICAL AND RELIGIOUS CONFLICT IN BRITAIN

3.5 Oliver Cromwell

During the Civil War **Oliver Cromwell** (Source A) emerged as the leading figure on the side of Parliament. He had become an MP in 1640, and by 1646 he was a very successful general and the idol of the army. He also had great political gifts. Therefore, he was an ideal link between the army and Parliament. It was his position in the army, however, that enabled Cromwell to increase his own power, as the generals, rather than Parliament, were actually in charge of the country. By the early 1650s Cromwell was clearly the most powerful man in the country, and in **1653** he was given a new title, the **Lord Protector of the Commonwealth of England**, a position he held until his death in **1658**.

Oliver Cromwell

The Restoration

After Cromwell's death his supporters quarrelled among themselves and were unable to govern the country firmly. By **1660** they decided to bring back the king. **Charles II**, the son of Charles I, agreed to rule on conditions which his father had always rejected, and he became King in May 1660. The return of the King is called **The Restoration**.

Cromwell's Influence

Cromwell was a deeply religious man and tried to instill **Puritan values** on everyday life in England.

As a general he believed that he was fighting God's battles, while in politics he was convinced that every decision he made had to reflect God's will. There is no doubt that his sincere religious beliefs influenced his actions in **Ireland** in **1649-1650** (see Source B).

Cromwell is one of the most important figures in the history of the British Isles. Yet unlike many of the other great figures in history he is remembered with little affection. The cruelty associated with his rule has influenced the way in which people think about him, but there is no doubt that Cromwell **changed** the course of English history. Parliament became more important, and the process by which power was transferred from the monarch to the people could not be stopped. One other consequence of Cromwell's rule was that future English governments were always careful to ensure that the army would never again become involved in politics.

ATTAINMENT TARGET 2: POINTS OF VIEW

3.5

The Effect of Cromwell's Rule in England and Wales.

England no longer had a King, and the House of Lords was abolished. In the Church, Bishops were abolished and each individual church was run by the minister and a committee elected by the congregation.

Nearly all previous forms of entertainment (dancing, fairs, etc.) were banned. Most of the people did not enjoy the strict conditions imposed by Puritan rule. Catholics were persecuted if they tried to practise their religion.

The Effect of Cromwell's Rule in Scotland.

The Scots were angered by Charles I's execution and they crowned his son, Prince Charles, as their King.

He then led an army into England in an attempt to regain the throne but was defeated by Cromwell.

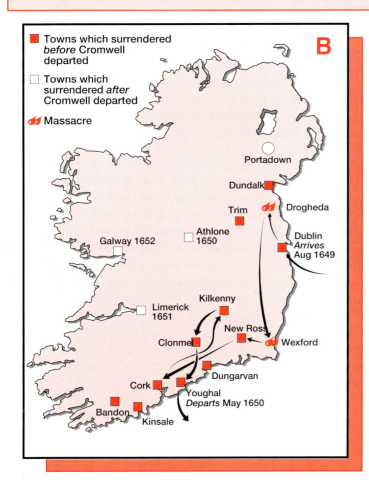

B

Cromwell's campaign in Ireland

?

1. Which groups of people in England and Scotland would have disliked the rules made by Cromwell about (a) religion and (b) entertainment?

2. What reasons do you think Cromwell would have given for making these changes?

POLITICAL AND RELIGIOUS CONFLICT IN BRITAIN

3.6 Cromwell's Campaign in Ireland

To understand why Cromwell came to Ireland we must look back to the Ulster Rebellion of 1641. This rebellion can be viewed in two ways -

(a) the Ulster Catholics who had been forced to surrender their lands to English and Scottish planters were striking back at the new Protestant settlers, and

(b) it became part of the Civil War as the Catholics in Ireland took the side of the King in his struggle against Parliament.

The Ulster rebellion resulted in the deaths of 10,000 to 15,000 Protestants, some of whom were massacred in particularly cruel incidents, such as at the River Bann near Portadown (see Sources A and B).

The stories of these massacres were greatly exaggerated and by the time the Puritans in the House of Commons were informed about these events, estimates of up to 300,000 Protestants being slaughtered were commonly believed in England. Parliament was determined that this rebellion should be crushed and it was decided that the cost of this exercise should be paid for by confiscating Irish land.

The Civil War in England meant that only a small force could be sent to Ireland in **1642** and the result was military stalemate (neither side being able to secure victory) for the next seven years. This was to change in **1649**, however, when following the king's execution, it was decided to send an army to Ireland to crush the enemies of the Commonwealth.

A

On a cold November day in 1641 ... a party of some 100 Protestant men, women and children who had been seized from their homes, robbed and stripped of most of their clothes, were herded together onto the bridge [at Portadown]. They were thrown or driven over the parapet into the water below where they were drowned or if they could swim were shot or knocked on the head as they came ashore.

From *Ireland - A History* by Robert Kee, 1980

Right: A seventeenth century artist's view of events at Portadown in 1641

?

1. Do you regard Source D as a reliable account of the events of 1649? Explain your answer.

2. What do sources A -D tell you about what it was like to live in Ireland in the 1640's?

3. What other evidence would you need to have to find out what life in the 1640's was like?

"Drowning men, women and children by hand: [gathering] upon bridges and casting them into rivers, who drowned not were killed with poles and shot with muskets" (adapted)

ATTAINMENT TARGET 3: USE OF EVIDENCE

3.6

C

[In 1649] *Oliver Cromwell was sent to Ireland to deal with the Catholic rebellion. The methods he used to crush the rebels were harsh. When English soldiers captured the garrison of the town of Drogheda they ran wild, killing nearly 3000 people (including 200 women).*

From *The Irish Question* by Hamish Macdonald, 1985.

ACTIVITY

Look at the statements below and say whether you believe them to be true or false. Give evidence from the sources to support your ideas.

1. In Portadown in 1641, the people who did not drown were attacked
2. In 1649 all the Catholics in Drogheda were killed by Cromwell
3. Women, the old and children were all attacked in Drogheda

Cromwell himself took charge of the army (12,000 men), and it landed at **Ringsend** near Dublin in **August 1649**. One of the first objectives for Cromwell's army was the town of **Drogheda**. It was occupied by a small force (a garrison), and after a very brief siege the town was stormed by Cromwell's troops in September 1649 after the walls had been breached by cannon fire. Most of the defending soldiers and many of the town's inhabitants were killed in this attack (see Sources C and D).

News of this slaughter spread quickly with the result that neighbouring Catholic towns surrendered to avoid a repeat of the events in Drogheda (See page 59 Source B).

Cromwell's actions in Drogheda have been fiercely criticised by subsequent generations of Irishmen. He himself saw the massacre as fair punishment for the murder of Protestants in 1641; indeed he judged the entire episode as a "righteous judgement of God upon these barbarous wretches."

After Drogheda Cromwell marched his troops south, and a similar attack took place on Wexford with many of the Catholic population being massacred. For Cromwell this had the desired effect as the neighbouring towns of New Ross, Cork, Bandon, Kinsale and Youghal quickly surrendered, once news of the events in Wexford reached them. Other towns surrendered in the spring of 1650 and although some fighting continued for a further two years, Cromwell was able to leave Ireland in 1650 in the knowledge that he had obtained a crushing victory over the Catholic rebels.

D

When the city was captured by the heretics, the blood of the Catholics was mercilessly shed in the streets, in the dwelling houses and in the open fields. To none was mercy shown; not to women, nor to the aged, nor to the young. The majority of the citizens became prey of the Parliamentary troops.

An eyewitness account of the attack on Drogheda by a Jesuit priest.

POLITICAL AND RELIGIOUS  CONFLICT IN BRITAIN

3.7 The Cromwellian Settlement

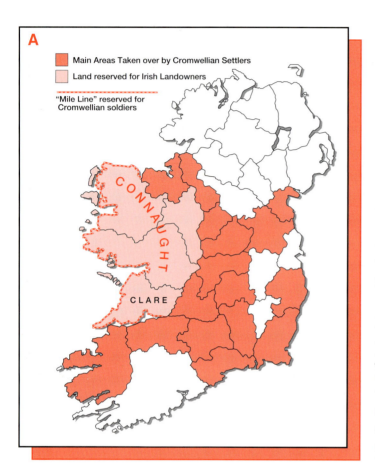

The Cromwellian Settlement of 1652

As well as taking revenge against the Irish Catholics for the rebellion they began in 1641, Cromwell knew he had an economic reason for having to conquer Ireland. The government in London needed money to repay loans which had been made during the English Civil War, and many officers in the New Model Army were owed huge amounts of back-pay. In place of money which the government did not have, Cromwell had already decided to pay these men with grants of land; land which was seized from the Catholic rebels after their defeat.

In fact, Cromwell's control of Ireland was guaranteed when nearly 35,000 Catholic soldiers left Ireland to join the armies of Catholic France and Spain. The English government hoped that its control over Ireland could be extended by a new scheme of plantation similar to the Ulster Plantation, but the attempt to attract large numbers of Protestant settlers to Ireland was a failure.

This meant that ordinary Catholics stayed in their homes, but their rents were paid to the new Protestant landowners. A number of Catholic landowners were allowed to keep some property, but they still had to leave their traditional lands and take instead much smaller and poorer holdings in the west. **County Clare** and most of the counties in **Connaught** were reserved for these Catholic landowners and their families. The West had, of course, the poorest farming land in Ireland, and the Catholics who were sent there were not allowed to live in towns or within three miles of the coast, as all coastal land was given to Cromwellian soldiers.

B

I meddle not with any man's conscience, but if by liberty of conscience you mean a liberty to exercise the Mass, I judge it best to use plain dealing, and let you know where the Parliament of England has power, that will not be allowed.

Cromwell's comments on the Catholic religion in Ireland

ATTAINMENT TARGET 1: CAUSE, CONSEQUENCE AND CHANGE

3.7

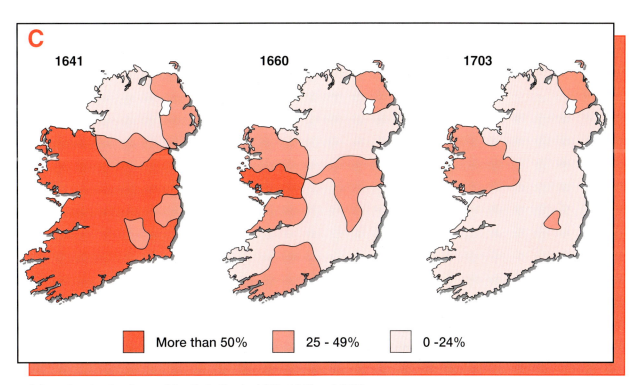

Maps showing land owned by Catholics in 1641, 1660 and 1703

1. Look at Source A. Why do you think Catholics were not allowed to live on the coast?

2. According to Source A, three areas, Ulster, Munster and south of Dublin, do not appear to be part of this settlement. Can you suggest any reasons for this?

3. Look at Source C. In which areas did Catholics continue to hold at least 25% of the land between 1641 and 1703?

4. Suggest why they lost land in other areas.

5. Did Catholics lose more land in the period 1641-1660 or in the period 1660-1703? Explain your conclusion.

The end result of the "Cromwellian Settlement" (1652) was the transfer of wealth and power to Protestants who now owned most of the land.

Not surprisingly, Cromwell's government in England, which was dominated by Puritans, did its utmost to make life very difficult for Catholics. Many were executed, while others were imprisoned or forced to leave the country. Indeed most of the Catholic clergy, numbering about 1,000 priests, were forced out of Ireland in the 1650s. When Charles II became king in 1660, he made very few changes to the Cromwellian land settlement, but he did relax the persecution of the Catholic Church in Ireland.

63

THE WILLIAMITE WARS

4.1 Europe in 1688

Europe in 1688

In 1688 war broke out in Europe between the French king, **Louis XIV**, and a league of European states, known as the **Grand Alliance**. This war lasted until 1697.

This Grand Alliance was led by **William of Orange** and consisted of the Spanish king whose Empire included the Spanish Netherlands; the Holy Roman Emperor who ruled the German states; and the rulers of Prussia and Bavaria. (See Source A above).

Some kings and rulers who were not members of the Grand Alliance wanted Louis defeated so that Europe could be at peace. **James II** of England did not join the alliance in 1688 as he felt that England was in no danger at that time. Besides, he wanted to remain on good terms with the Dutch and the French. James had become king of England in 1685 and, even though he was a Catholic, no one really objected to him. However, there was one small rebellion led by the Duke of Monmouth. After this, James kept a large army and also promoted many Catholics to

ATTAINMENT TARGET 1: CAUSE, CONSEQUENCE AND CHANGE

4.1

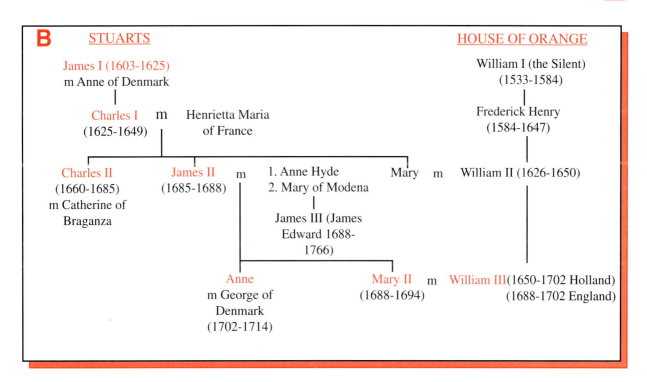

The Stuart and Orange Family Trees

officer status. He tried to introduce forms of religious toleration for non-Anglicans (people who were not members of the Church of England). Parliament became increasingly suspicious of him and feared that he was trying to make England a Catholic country. There was also concern that he may persecute Protestants as Louis XIV was doing in France. James's heir to the throne was his elder daughter, **Mary**, who was married to William of Orange.

In June 1688, however, James's second wife, **Mary of Modena**, had a son. This changed things dramatically. The boy - who was a Catholic - would succeed his father, displacing his two older Protestant sisters, Mary and Anne. To prevent a Catholic becoming king, the English parliament invited William of Orange, Mary's husband, to take the English throne.

William landed on the south coast of England in November 1688 and moved to London. James II, with his wife and son, fled to France. William and Mary were made joint monarchs in February 1689. This is known as the **Glorious Revolution**. William had been eager to come to England, because he hoped to add English support to his struggle against Louis XIV. However, he soon found that his attention was diverted to events in Ireland.

?

Using the information in this unit, explain the reasons why Parliament believed that William had the best claim to the English throne in 1688.

THE WILLIAMITE WARS

4.2 James II and Ireland

A

December 1688: Frequently, before the siege actually commenced, we had been alarmed by reports that the Roman Catholics intended to rise in arms against us and to act over the tragedy of 1641 ... At last a regiment of them raised by the Marquis of Antrim, actually arrived at Newtownlimavady, on their march to Derry ... These set us immediately to consider what was to be done; but we could not determine among ourselves what was best.

While we were in this confused hesitation, on 7th December 1688, a few resolute apprentice boys determined for us. These ran to the Gates and shut them, drew up the bridge, and seized the magazine. This, like magic, roused an unanimous spirit of defence and now with one voice we determined to maintain the city at all hazards, and each sex and age joined in the important cause.

Thomas Ashe (A Protestant from Co. Londonderry)

B

December 1688: The first of Ireland's Protestants who appeared for the Prince of Orange were the inhabitants of Londonderry.

The burgesses hearing thereof, and that the King was abandoned by his army and by the people of England, did resolutely, about the beginning of December 1688, shut up their gates against the said regiment.

... About the same time the viceroy sent two companies to be quartered at Enniskillen, a small inland town in the same province. This also refused entrance to the King's garrison.

Nicholas Plunkett (Contemporary Jacobite author and supporter of Tyrconnell).

Ireland was still ruled by England in the late 17th century and the land was divided among the various settlers and the native Catholic population. The result of the Cromwellian Settlement (1652) was to divide Irish society into landowners on one side and a great number of small tenant-farmers, called cottiers, on the other.

During James's reign much had been done to improve the position for Catholics just as had happened in England. Many former landowners also hoped that James would restore their estates to them. In **1687** James had made his brother-in-law, **Richard Talbot**, the king's representative in Ireland. His official title was **Lord Lieutenant**, but he was also known as the **Earl of Tyrconnell**, or even as "Lying Dick". He strengthened the Irish army in case it was needed to support James. In 1688 Tyrconnell sent troops to Ulster, but the garrisons in Derry and Enniskillen would not admit them. Protestants in Ireland declared their support for William and Mary and prepared to fight for them. Those who supported William are usually call **Williamites**, while James's supporters are known as **Jacobites**. A leading Ulster Jacobite was the **Earl of Antrim**.

ATTAINMENT TARGET 3: USE OF EVIDENCE

4.2

C

Finding the people of Londonderry continue obstinate to their rebellion, and that there appears no likelyhood of reducing them by fair means, I desire your lordship to give orders presently, to all the companies of your regiment, to be in readiness to march at an hour's warning, it being my resolution in case I doe not hear, by Friday's post, that the Citty of Derry has submitted, to order them, with severall other regiments of horse, foot and dragoons, to march against it, and will soon follow them myself.

I am, My Lord yr ldps most faythfull humble servant.

Tyrconnell

Above: Letter from Earl of Tyrconnell to the Earl of Antrim, 1688

Right: James VII and II, by Sir Peter Lely

1. Sources A, B and C are all primary evidence. How useful are they to an historian?

2. Which sentences in Source A show a change in the attitude of the people of Derry?

3. How does Source B differ from Source A in its description of the closure of the gates? Suggest a reason for this difference.

4. Do the differences between Sources A and B mean that they are unreliable? Explain your answer.

5. Why do you think the word 'rebellion' was used in Source C to describe events in Derry?

THE WILLIAMITE WARS

4.3 The Williamite Wars

James arrived in Ireland in March 1689, landing at **Kinsale** and arriving in **Dublin** on **24 March**. By that time many groups of Protestants throughout Ulster were fighting back. When they were unsuccessful, many fled to England or Scotland, while some took refuge in fortified towns such as Derry.

This quarrel which was emerging between Louis XIV, James II and William III became known as the **War of the Three Kings**, and lasted from 1688 - 1691.

These boxes tell you about the main people involved in the Williamite Wars.

James II 1685-1688
Tried to turn England into a Catholic state. Suspended the Penal Laws in Ireland. Expanded his fleet of ships. Retired to France on a pension of a million livres (£1 million) per year.

William III 1689-1702
Always opposed France. Believed the safety of European states lay in their joint co-operation against France. Married to Mary, James II's elder daughter.

Tyrconnell 1630-1691
Real name Richard Talbot; nicknamed "Lying Dick". Served in the French army in Europe. Lord Lieutenant in Ireland and in charge of the Irish army. Brother of James' wife, Mary of Modena.

Ginkel
A Williamite Lieutenant-General. Known also as First Earl of Athlone. Took charge in Ireland when William left in 1691. Fought at the Battle of Aughrim.

Patrick Sarsfield
A Jacobite officer. Defender of Limerick. In August 1690, he destroyed a siege-train at Ballineedy near Limerick. Made Earl of Lucan on Tyrconnell's recommendation.

Schomberg
A Williamite general. Landed at Carrickfergus in August 1690 and besieged the town. Killed at Old Bridge near the Boyne, but exactly how he was killed remains unclear.

ATTAINMENT TARGET 2: POINTS OF VIEW

4.3

Williamites

36,000 men including Blue Dutch Guards, Danes, German Brandenburgers, French Protestants. These soldiers were well trained mercenaries. Good artillery - 50-60 large canon and several mortars. Up to date flintlock muskets and bayonets.

Jacobites

25,000 men of whom 6,000 were French who had been in battle before. The rest were inexperienced. No canon. 12 French field pieces. The soldiers had scythes or sharpened sticks.

Left and above: the opposing forces compared.

Right: William III

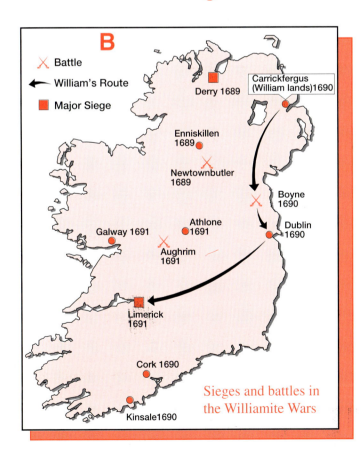

Sieges and battles in the Williamite Wars

?

1. What is a mercenary?

2. What are the advantages and disadvantages of having mercenaries on your side in a battle?

3. Name two problems which may occur in an army consisting of various nationalities.

4. Using the information given about the leaders and the relative strengths of the forces, which side do you think had the best chance of winning? Give reasons for your answers.

69

THE WILLIAMITE WARS

4.4 The Siege of Derry

In the last unit we read how the apprentice boys of Derry had shut the gates against the advancing Jacobite army in December 1688. To some people in the city of Derry this was seen as treason against their lawful king, James. For others, this action was vital for their security.

When James arrived in Ireland in **March 1689**, he was determined to crush all remaining opposition. One his first actions was to demand the surrender of Derry, the Williamite stronghold which was then under the command of **Colonel Lundy**. This marked the beginning of the siege which would

A

Our drink was nothing but water, which we paid very dear for, and could not get without danger.

George Walker,
Governor of Derry.

The Siege of Derry 1689

B

Everyday some ... deserted the garrison, so that the enemy received constant intelligence of our proceedings This gave some trouble and made us remove our ammunition very often ... Our iron-ball is now all spent, and instead of them we make balls of brick, cast over with lead, to the weight and size of our iron-ball.

George Walker,
Governor of Derry.

last 105 days. Governor Lundy and the city council considered surrendering. He was discredited for this and forced to leave. The **Rev George Walker** became the new Governor of the city. On **4 June 1689** a boom was placed across the Foyle leaving those defending the city cut off and running very short of supplies.

The Jacobites were short of heavy artillery, but they increased the weight of shot fired.

ACTIVITY

In groups, you are reporters for a 1689 version of "News at Ten". Construct a report from the City of Derry, describing living conditions there and the difficulties experienced by the besieging Jacobite forces.

ATTAINMENT TARGET 1: CAUSE, CONSEQUENCE AND CHANGE

4.4

D

Date	Big	Small
April 24-27	0	17
April 27-6 May	0	6
June 2-21-July	261	326
July 22	0	42
July 23	0	20

Canon shot or mortars used against the City of Derry in 1689.

E

... the cold which the men — specially the women and children contracted, hereby, added to their want of rest and food, occasional diseases in the garrison, as fevers, flux, etc. of which great numbers died.

John Mackenzie (Presbyterian Chaplin to Walker's Regiment.)

F

Horse flesh sold for 8d per pound	
A quarter of a dog	5s 6d
A dog's head	2s 6d
A cat	4s 6d
A pound of tallow	4s 0d
A pound of salted hides	1s 0d
A quarter of horse blood	1s 0d
A rat	1s 0d
A mouse	0s 6d
A horse pudding	0s 6d
A handful of chick weed	0s 1d
A quart meal when found	1s 0d

Prices of food during the Siege of Derry (1s = 5p; 6d = 2½p)

Conditions in the city deteriorated. Look at Sources A to F and you will see that the defenders were short of ammunition food and supplies. They were also subjected to many diseases (Source E).

A relief force arrived in Lough Foyle on 13 June but did not try to break through the boom. The ship's captain claimed that when he had not heard from the city's defenders, he assumed they did not need his help. Eventually on **28 July** the ship's captain, Major-General Kirke, was told by London to break the boom. The ship called **The Mountjoy** broke the boom, ending the siege. The Irish/Jacobite army left as quickly as possible. Both armies suffered heavy casualties.

While the siege was taking place in Derry, the garrison at **Enniskillen** intercepted the Jacobites at Newtownbutler and forced the Jacobites to divide their forces, keeping half the Jacobite army from going to Derry.

In August William's general, **Schomberg** landed at Carrickfergus, captured it after a brief siege and soon all of Ulster was in Williamite hands.

?

1. List the problems experienced by those inside the city during the siege.

2. Explain why you think the citizens of Derry were prepared to put up with these conditions.

THE WILLIAMITE WARS

4.5 The Battle of the Boyne

A modern Orange banner showing King William crossing the Boyne

B

The day was very clear, as if the Sun itself had a mind to see what would happen.

George Story, a Chaplain in Schomberg's army.

At the beginning of March 1690 four thousand Danes arrived in Belfast to help William. Within a week more reinforcements had arrived from England. Many of the Danes were keen to end the war in Ireland and bring William back to once again take charge of the Grand Alliance in the European conflict. At the same time Louis XIV agreed to send James some battle-hardened French soldiers. Louis wanted the war to continue in Ireland so that William would be kept out of the European conflict.

In June 1690 **William** arrived at **Carrickfergus** and marched on Dundalk. King James moved north from Dublin to meet him. On **1st July 1690** the two armies met at the **River Boyne** in Co Meath.

ACTIVITY

Use the library and any other books available to find pictures of William and James at the Boyne. Suggest why many differences appear in these pictures.

ATTAINMENT TARGET 1: CAUSE, CONSEQUENCE AND CHANGE

4.5

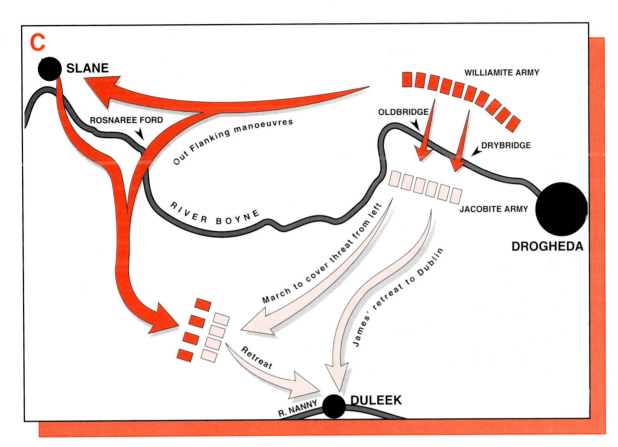

The Battle of the Boyne, 1st July 1690

James believed that William's main attack would come from Rosnaree so he moved more than half of his army in that direction. However, at that point the ground was marshy and no fighting was to take place there.

Instead the Williamite army crossed between Oldbridge and Drybridge. The Duke of Schomberg and the Rev George Walker were killed there.

Although the Jacobites were heavily outnumbered the battle lasted for two hours. William's army crossed the river first and the Jacobite cavalry fought well. When James saw that the battle was lost, he fled with his bodyguard to Dublin, before setting sail for France. The Jacobite losses numbered about 1300, while the Williamites lost about 400.

Because William was part of the European Grand Alliance, there was rejoicing throughout Europe that he had defeated an ally of Louis XIV's.

> **?**
> 1. List the reasons why William was victorious at the Boyne.
> 2. Which reason do you think was the most important and why?

THE WILLIAMITE WARS

4.6 Limerick and Aughrim

Seventeenth century siege guns in use:
top - firing
centre - cooling the barrel
bottom - cooling the breech with sheepskins soaked in water.

After the Battle of the Boyne, Tyrconnell was prepared to negotiate with William. However, some other Jacobites such as Sarsfield refused to do so. They hoped for better peace terms from William if they could hold out for longer. The rest of the Irish army was concentrated in Limerick and Athlone. Early in August 1690 William laid siege to Limerick. **Patrick Sarsfield** led the defenders in Limerick. He managed to intercept and destroy a great quantity of William's guns at Ballineedy.

Although William was still able to launch an attack on Limerick, the Jacobites were able to hold out.

As autumn and the heavy rains set in, William finally gave up and left Ireland. He left **General Ginkel** in charge. Ginkel offered peace to Sarsfield and the Jacobites. They rejected this, however, and decided to fight on. Ginkel then prepared for a final assault. The Jacobites were now led by the **Marquis St Ruth**.

B

William, having made a larger breach in the wall, gave a general assault which lasted for three hours; and though his men mounted the breach, and some even entered the town, they were gallantly repulsed and forced to retire with considerable loss.

Charles O'Kelly, a Gaelic Irishman, speaking about the siege at Limerick.

C

The Irish ventured upon the breach again, and from the walls and every place so pester'd us upon the counterscarp, that after nigh three hours resisting bullets, stones, broken bottles ... and whatever way could be thought on to destroy us, our ammunition being spent, it was judged safest to return to our trenches.

George Story, a Williamite.

1. In what ways do the accounts in Sources B and C of the last days of the siege differ?

2. How do you account for these differences?

3. "Any historical source is useful to an historian". Do you agree? Refer to the sources and the map in this unit in your answer.

ATTAINMENT TARGET 3: USE OF EVIDENCE

4.6

The Battle of Aughrim, 12 July 1691

By the summer of 1691 the Jacobites were at Aughrim blocking Ginkel's approach to Galway. Sarsfield suggested that the Jacobite army withdraw to Limerick, but St Ruth had the stronger position in higher ground, while the Williamites would have to cross a bog. However, the Williamites had twice as many heavy guns and Ginkel gave the order to attack, even though his men had just completed a long march.

St Ruth was killed in battle and this left the Jacobites in disarray. Most of their forces retreated to Limerick. Ginkel followed them there and it seemed as though there would be another long siege. However, the failure of French help to arrive and the sudden death of **Tyrconnell** persuaded other Jacobite leaders to agree to Ginkel's peace terms. Consequently, the Jacobites surrendered on **26 September 1691** and a treaty was signed in **October 1691**.

The Battle of Aughrim 12 July 1691.

THE WILLIAMITE WARS

4.7 The Treaty of Limerick

The peace agreed to at Limerick in **October 1691** contained civil and military terms.

> **Civil:**
> 1. The property of Jacobite landowners who still held arms in Limerick would not be confiscated.
> 2. Irish Catholics were allowed to practise their religion.
> 3. Almost 1,000,000 acres of land belonging to Catholics was confiscated and given to William's supporters.
> 4. Ginkel was made Earl of Athlone and given 26,480 acres of land.

> **Military:**
> Irish Jacobite soldiers were offered three choices:
> (a) They could return to their homes in peace.
> (b) They could join the Williamite army and serve with it in Europe against France.
> (c) They could go to France to fight for King James, in alliance with King Louis XIV, against William and his European allies.
>
> If a soldier chose option (c) he would be given free transport to France, in English ships, with his wife and children.

Many Jacobite soldiers chose option (c), and at the end of 1691 almost 12,000 soldiers went to France in ships provided by Ginkel, or in French ships which had arrived in Ireland just after the siege of Limerick.

These exiles are known as **The Wild Geese**, and they fought as the army of King James in Europe until 1697. After peace was restored in Europe many of them became part of the French army. **Patrick Sarsfield** was the most famous of these "Wild Geese". He was killed in battle in 1693 in the Austrian Netherlands.

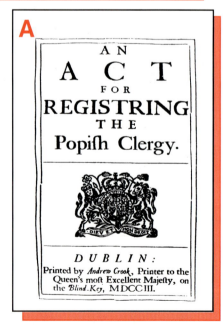

Right: An example of a cover for a Penal Law

ATTAINMENT TARGET 1: CAUSE, CONSEQUENCE AND CHANGE

4.7

The Penal Laws

A series of laws was passed after 1691, mainly by the Irish Parliament. These laws had two main purposes.

(a) To convert as many of the Irish Catholics as possible, especially the landowning class, to the Protestant religion.

(b) To exclude all those who remained Catholic from …

   (i) the right to carry arms.

   (ii) all professions except the medical.

   (iii) political power at local and national level.

   (iv) the possession of landed property except in a short-term lease hold basis.

   (v) all education except that which endeavoured to convert them to Protestantism.

   (vi) owning a horse worth more than £5.

Some Catholics did change their religion to avoid penalties, though most remained Catholic. Similar laws were applied in England, but as Catholics were in a minority, these laws had only limited effect there.

After 1728 Catholics were not allowed to vote at elections. If a son became a Protestant, he automatically became owner of his Catholic father's estate, even if his father was still alive.

Catholics were not the only religious group to suffer. Presbyterians discovered that they were also to be denied many rights. Their ministers could preach freely but could not perform marriage ceremonies. In 1704 Presbyterians were also banned from town councils and from holding other official positions.

B

> ARTICLES
> Civil and Military,
> Agreed upon the 3d. Day of *Octob.* 1691.
> BETWEEN
> The Right Honourable, Sir *Charles Porter*, Knight, and *Thomas Coningsby*, Esq; Lords Justices of *Ireland*; and His Excellency the Baron *De Ginckle*, Lieutenant General, and Commander in Chief of the *English* Army, On the One Part.
> AND
> The Right Honourable, *Patrick*, Earl of *Lucan*, *Piercy* Viscount *Gallmoy*, Collonel *Nicholas Purcel*, Collonel *Nicholas Cusack*, Sir *Toby Butler*, Collonel *Garret Dillon*, and Collonel *John Brown*, On the other Part. In the Behalf of the *Irish* Inhabitants, in the City and County of *Lymerick*, the Counties of *Clare*, *Kerry*, *Cork*, *Sligo*, and *Mayo*.

Extract from The Treaty of Limerick 1691

ACTIVITY
Design a cover for a Penal Law mentioned in this unit. (Source A is an example.)

?

1. Choose four consequences of the Williamite wars, outlined in this unit.

2. Place these in order of importance. Give reasons for the order you have chosen.

3. How did life for Catholics and Presbyterians in Ireland change as a result of these Penal Laws?

THE WILLIAMITE WARS

4.8 The Jacobites

When Queen Anne died in 1714, the Elector of Hanover became **King George I** of England. If James' son had been restored to the throne, England would have had a Catholic king and an earlier Act of Succession had forbidden this. Many who had previously fought for Spain decided to join James's son, **James Edward**, who believed he had a claim to the throne. He was referred to as **The Pretender**.

Had this young James been prepared to turn Protestant, he may have become king, because the new King George was unattractive and did not even speak English. When James II died in 1701, Louis XIV of France promised to help James' son.

In 1715 there was more talk of a Jacobite rising, but this time there was less hope of French help as Louis XIV had died. However, James Edward, now aged 27, was determined to attempt to regain the English throne.

At first the rising went well, but the **Earl of Mar**, who had roused the Scottish clans, was not a good military leader. The English government had sent Dutch troops to help the Duke of Argyll who was fighting Mar and the Jacobites. The government forces outnumbered the Jacobites by three to one, but heavy snow prevented an immediate attack in late November or early December.

James Edward had a very cold and reserved personality, and when, on 22 December 1715 he landed at Peterhead he was not very optimistic and said: "For me it is no new thing to be unfortunate, since my whole life from my cradle has been a constant series of misfortunes."

When news reached the Jacobites that Argyll was coming to attack at the end of January 1715, James Edward and Mar escaped to France, leaving their followers to look after themselves.

When George II succeeded his father to the English throne in 1727, relations between England and Scotland were still very poor.

The Stuart and Hanoverian Family Trees

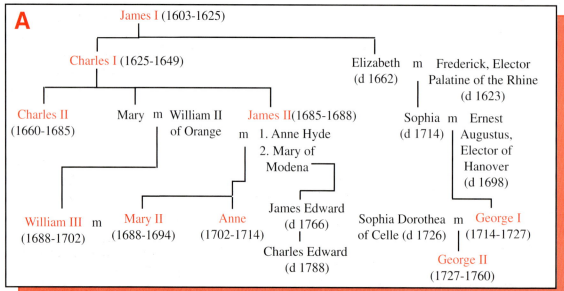

ATTAINMENT TARGET !: CAUSE, CONSEQUENCE AND CHANGE

4.8

Prince Charles Edward Stuart, Bonnie Prince Charlie

By 1745 the Jacobites were more hopeful of success because James Edward's elder son, **Prince Charles Edward**, was a young man of energy and courage, and he was very popular. He is known as **Bonnie Prince Charlie**.

He sold his family jewels to raise the necessary capital, bought two ships and sailed from Nantes for Scotland. He was not greeted with enthusiasm, although some did rally to his cause and raised the standard to his father, James, at Glenfinnan on 19 August 1745. After this, he did gain support and it seemed as if he would be successful; a notable victory was won at **Prestonpans**. Charles was hoping for French support. The French sent supplies and money, but no men. Charles, determined to fight on, marched towards London at the beginning of November 1745. In London there was panic and the king was planning to flee to Hanover. Charles's advisors, however, persuaded him not to advance but to return to Scotland and launch a new campaign in the spring.

When they returned to Scotland, they found many Scots very unwelcoming. Charles gathered about 5000 troops on **Culloden Moor**, near Inverness in April 1746, but they were massacred by the superior government forces led by the Duke of Cumberland.

For the next five months, Bonnie Prince Charlie, who had escaped the massacre, lived as a fugitive with a £30,000 price on his head. He was never captured by the government troops as he was protected by many Scots including **Flora MacDonald**. On 19 September 1746 he was picked up by a French frigate and taken back to exile.

The Jacobite threat to the throne had finally ended.

> **?**
> Why do you think the Jacobite threat to the English throne was unsuccessful?

Index

America   32 - 37
Argyll, Duke of   78
Armada, Spanish   24 - 31
Aughrim, Battle of   75

Babington, Anthony   20
Boleyn, Anne   16, 18
Bonnie Prince Charlie *see Charles Edward, Prince*
Bothwell, Earl of   16
Boyne, Battle of   72 - 73

Cadiz   26
Calais   27, 29
Castlehaven, Lord   46
Cavaliers   56, 57
Charles I   46, 50, 54 - 57
Charles II   50, 58, 63
Charles V (Emperor)   12
Charles IX (France)   10
Charles Edward, Prince   79
Chichester, Sir Arthur   42 - 46
Civil War   54 - 57
Commonwealth (1649-1660)   50, 58 - 59, 60
Cromwell, Oliver   50, 58 - 63
Cromwellian land settlement   62 - 63, 66
Culloden Moor, Battle of   79
Cumberland, Duke of   79

Darnley, Lord   16, 19
Derry   43, 66, 67, 70 - 71
Drake, Sir Francis   22, 26
Drogheda   61

Edward VI   24
Elizabeth I   12, 15 - 18, 20 - 22, 24, 27, 31, 40

Fawkes, Guy   52 - 53
Flight of the Earls   42

George I   78
George II   78
Ginkel (Earl of Athlone)   68, 74, 75, 76

Girona   28, 30
Golden Hind   22, 23
Gunpowder Plot   52 - 53

Habsburgs   12
Henry VII   24
Henry VIII   12, 18, 24
Holy Roman Empire   7, 10, 12 - 13
Huguenots   12

Jacobites   66 - 78
James I   16, 50, 51, 52
James II   64, 68, 72 - 73, 76, 78
James V (Scotland)   14, 16
James Edward   78
Jamestown   36 - 37

Kirk O'Fields   17
Knox, John   15

Laud, Archbishop   51
Limerick, Siege of   74
         Treaty of   76
Louis XIV (France)   64, 72 - 73, 78
Lundy, Colonel   70
Luther, Martin   9

Mary I (of England)   12, 15, 18, 24
Mary II (Stuart/Orange)   65
Mary of Guise   14
Mary of Modena   65
Mary, Queen of Scots   12, 14 - 21
Medina Sidonia, Duke of   26, 27
Mellifont, Treaty of   40
Monea Castle   45
Monmouth, Duke of   64
Mountjoy, Lord   40, 46

New Model Army   56, 57, 62

Omagh   46 - 47
O'Neill, Hugh   40, 42, 46
Ottoman Empire   7, 8, 9

Parliamentarians   54 - 55
Penal Laws   77
Pilgrim Fathers   51
Philip II (of Spain)   23 - 27
Plantation   32 -49
Pope   19, 25
Presbyterians   48
Protestantism   8 - 9, 23, 41, 62
Puritans   49, 51, 54, 58, 60

Rebellion of 1641   49, 60 - 61, 62, 66
Rizzio   16 - 17
Roundheads   56, 57
Royalists   54 - 57

St Bartholomew's Day Massacre   13
St Ruth   74 - 75
Santa Cruz   26
Sarsfield, Patrick   68, 74, 76
Schomberg   68, 71, 73
Smith, John   36 - 37

Talbot, Richard   66 - 68, 74, 75
Torture   24 - 25
Tyrconnell, *see Talbot, Richard*
Tyrone, Earl of *see O'Neill*

Ulster Plantation   40 - 49

Walker, Rev George   70
Walsingham, Sir Francis   20
Wild Geese, The   76
William I (The Silent)   23
William of Orange 20, 64 -66, 68, 69, 72 - 75
Williamites   66 - 77